Advance
A Simple Book of [...]

"Danny Kofke's book, *A Simple Book of Financial Wisdom*, is a winner. It lays out in very simple terms a solid, wise approach to managing personal finances. It is particularly timely during these times of financial crisis. It offers hope and relief."

Juan Williams
JOURNALIST, POLITICAL ANALYST FOR FOX NEWS CHANNEL AND AUTHOR OF
MUZZLED: THE ASSAULT ON HONEST DEBATE

"The new economic reality facing so many people requires a disciplined approach to money management. In this book, Mr. Kofke gives key principles for building a strong financial foundation from an early age, and it is truly a must-read for everyone ready to take control of their finances."

Samuel T. Jackson
FOUNDER, CHAIRMAN & CEO, ECONOMIC EMPOWERMENT INITIATIVE, INC. AND MEMBER
OF PRESIDENT OBAMA'S ADVISORY COUNCIL ON FINANCIAL CAPABILITY

"Danny Kofke doesn't just talk about finances, he practices what he preaches. *A Simple Book of Financial Wisdom* is a great read and so important in these times. Even more important is the message for children. In today's world the simple messages are the best."

Martha Zoller
HOST OF THE MARTHA ZOLLER SHOW AND NAMED ONE OF THE "HEAVY HUNDRED"
TALK SHOW HOSTS IN AMERICA BY *TALKERS MAGAZINE*

"I can't imagine a better book on how to live 'richly' on a modest salary. Danny's story is inspiring and his lessons invaluable. His advice is solid, simple, and sound."

Kimberly Palmer
AUTHOR OF *GENERATION EARN* AND PERSONAL FINANCE COLUMNIST
AT *US NEWS & WORLD REPORT*

"Your book is an inspiration to anyone trying to save money and live on less."

Dr. Pat Robertson
HOST OF *THE 700 CLUB* AND FOUNDER OF *THE CHRISTIAN
BROADCASTING NETWORK*

"If every American had read Danny Kofke's book before 2005, the housing collapse and economic recession of 2008 would have never happened. Danny's commonsense approach to a family's financial management is a recipe for peace of mind and a happy life. I am buying the book for all my grandchildren."

U.S. Senator **Johnny Isakson**

"Danny Kofke gives tips and tools vital to get by in tough economic times. Whether single or trying to support a family of four, anyone living on a modest income will find something of value here. Make his book part of your library."

Neale S. Godfrey
CEO & Chairman Children's Financial Network, Inc.

"When looking for advice about wise money use, who better to ask than someone who practices what he preaches? Danny and his wife made the choice to have one at-home parent and thus are raising their two children on his teacher's salary. (Yep, that's him riding his bike to work and carrying a brown-bag lunch.) With friendly, conversational language Danny shows how not just to stretch a dollar, but how to derive true value from it. Danny's focus is on building the life you want by using money in ways that reflect your personal values, and your dreams."

Donna Freedman
MSN Money personal finance columnist

"Danny Kofke's book illustrates so simply what each of us—and our children—should know and practice when it comes to creating financial success in our lives. The concepts are not hard, and Danny's application of them shows that with simple awareness comes great rewards."

Dale A. Alexander
CLU, ChFC, CFP, president Alexander & Company

"Danny Kofke has written a heartfelt and sensible book for those who want to accomplish more with their money. His wise advice is fun to read and will show you how to live wealthy no matter how much or how little you have."

Laura Adams
author of *Money Girl's Smart Moves to Grow Rich*

"Danny Kofke nails it on the head. Being wealthy doesn't make you happy. He focuses on recognizing what you do have. People get into financial trouble when they don't know how they're spending their money. Practical, easy to read and understand with real life examples."

Bill Faiferlick
FINANCIAL STRATEGIST, AUTHOR & TALK SHOW HOST

"Rarely can you find someone to walk you through how they paid off debt, are saving for emergencies, preparing for retirement and teaching their children about money. It's also refreshing to hear how marriage and money conversations can be peaceful and exciting as two people work together to manage their money wisely. Danny has provided people a treasure with his new book. No, you won't find magic formulas, but you will find personal finance that make sense, and that is straightforward, for anyone to implement in their lives."

Jason Price
PERSONAL FINANCE BLOGGER AT ONEMONEYDESIGN.COM

"*A Simple Book of Financial Wisdom* is a gem of a read. You'll step away with a crystal clear understanding of the basics of money and a checklist of easy steps to follow to achieve financial freedom. By the time you are done reading this slim, powerful book you will have the knowledge and the inspiration to help you (and your children) truly live the life you want to live. Buy this book today. It will pay dividends for years to come."

Manisha Thakor
CO-AUTHOR OF *ON MY OWN TWO FEET* AND *GET FINANCIALLY NAKED*

"Danny Kofke's book, *A Simple Book of Financial Wisdom*, is a wakeup call. We are living in a day of financial crisis and this book offers you the financial skills to obtain freedom and help you plan a future that can bring greater security for you, your children and even your grandchildren. Why do I especially like this book? Because it doesn't just talk about the problem it gives you solutions in very practical ways to meet the financial problems you're facing."

Dr. Marilyn Hickey
PRESIDENT, MARILYN HICKEY MINISTRIES

"A must-read for every parent and grandparent to read first, and then to pass on these 're-learned' financial fundamentals and principles to the future generations of our nation."

Rick Durkee

HOST OF MONEY MATTERS 94.3WSC FM CHARLESTON SC, FOUNDER OF THE COASTAL FINANCIAL PLANNING GROUP

"Drastic situations sometimes call for simple solutions. In these dire financial times, Danny Kofke offers just that. *A Simple Book of Financial Wisdom* is a perfect primer for helping people get their financial houses in order and a reminder to all of us that there's a lot more to happiness than money and stuff."

Jeff Yeager

AUTHOR, *THE CHEAPSKATE NEXT DOOR* AND *THE ULTIMATE CHEAPSKATE'S ROAD MAP TO TRUE RICHES*

"Danny Kofke is living proof that you can be happy and live well without pulling down a six-figure income. Best of all, he generously shares how he manages that in *A Simple Book of Financial Wisdom*. I enjoyed his first book, and absolutely love this one."

Gerri Detweiler

PERSONAL FINANCE EXPERT AND CO-AUTHOR OF FIVE BOOKS INCLUDING *REDUCE DEBT, REDUCE STRESS*

"*A Simple Book of Financial Wisdom* isn't really simple after all. It provides, not just a sense of how much more you could do with what you have, but a moral perspective about what's really important. He reminds you how having only modest means doesn't keep you from being happy. And he does it without the usual browbeating, emotional bullying or guilt-tripping. With the country still digging out from years of ignoring consequences, this is a timely, useful story to tell."

Michael E. Kanell

ECONOMICS WRITER, *THE ATLANTA JOURNAL-CONSTITUTION,* AND CO-AUTHOR OF *PRESIMETRICS*

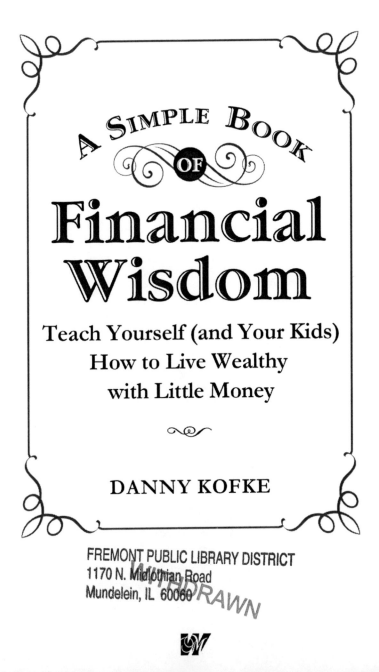

A SIMPLE BOOK OF

Financial Wisdom

Teach Yourself (and Your Kids) How to Live Wealthy with Little Money

DANNY KOFKE

A Simple Book of Financial Wisdom
Teach Yourself (and Your Kids) How to Live Wealthy with Little Money

Danny Kofke

ISBN: 978-1-936214-45-7
Library of Congress Control Number: 2011934919

Edited by Lisa Pliscou
Proofread by Karen Kibler
Index by Jean Jesensky, Endswell Indexing

Wyatt-MacKenzie Publishing
DEADWOOD, OREGON
www.WyattMacKenzie.com

Publisher's Cataloging-in-Publication data

Kofke, Danny.
    A simple book of financial wisdom : teach yourself (and your kids) how to
live wealthy with little money / Danny Kofke.
    p. cm.
    Includes bibliographical references and index.
    ISBN 978-1-936214-45-7

1. Finance —Personal. 2. Families — Economic aspects. 3. Money. 4. Investments. 5. Consumer education. I. Title.

HG179 .K64 2011
332.024 —dc22   2011934919

Contents

INTRODUCTION
How This Book Came to Be

When I wrote my first book *How to Survive (and perhaps thrive) on a Teacher's Salary* in 2007, I never imagined it would get as much exposure as it has. My original goal was for it to be something for my family and friends to read; I never actually intended on having it published.

A few of my colleagues had told me that my wife Tracy and I did well with our finances and that I should write a book describing how we did this. I didn't give too much thought to the idea until a year later, when Tracy and our six-month-old daughter Ava were out of town. I'm not great with idle time and I think the Man Upstairs put it in my head to sit down and start writing. So I did. A few months later, my book was complete.

— *My Media Journey* —

Much of my success with the media for *How to Survive* had to do with my perseverance. I pitched many producers (sometimes numerous times) early in the mornings, before I left to go to school and teach. I started off small and had some interviews with local radio shows and my hometown newspaper.

Then in January 2008 I saw on my local NBC affiliate that they had a "classroom connection" segment they aired once a week. I researched the program and emailed the reporter. She responded pretty fast and set up a date to come and film me in my classroom. I was so excited and extremely nervous when they interviewed me about my book and filmed me working with some of my students.

I continued to give interviews with various print media and on radio shows over the next couple of years. I had my first in-studio interview on Fox Atlanta's *Good Day Atlanta* morning television show in October 2008.

The Recession Catapults Me into National Media

During the later part of 2008 our country experienced an economic downturn. Many people were forced to live on less than they were used to—this is where my message and book fit in.

In January 2010, I had my first national television interview on *Fox & Friends*. I went to their studio in Atlanta and conducted it via satellite. One of the hosts, Steve Doocy, and I discussed ways to save money. They introduced me as a teacher and author of the book *How to Survive (and Perhaps Thrive) on a Teacher's Salary* and flashed a picture of my book for all of America to see. At this point I started to realize that I was becoming an "expert" on personal finance. I thought that many of the things my family did were pretty much common sense and that most people were doing them too, but I was wrong. After getting this call from Fox I realized there was a strong need for me to share my basic financial information with others.

The next month I was invited to appear on CNN's *Newsroom* with Fredericka Whitfield. The subject of this interview was "thriving on $39,000 a year." I was becoming more and more at ease while being interviewed. In addition, I found it much easier to talk with someone in person rather than on a satellite feed, although eventually I got much more comfortable with this as I went along.

Some Highlights Along the Way

I was then able to appear on *The 700 Club* (I think a higher power definitely had a hand in this). Shortly after my book came out, I emailed a producer from *The 700 Club* and she responded that I wasn't a good fit for them. Two years later, after I had been on a few television shows, I decided to follow up with this same producer again. This time she responded immediately and said yes. I feel this happened for a couple of reasons. First, money management was a hot topic now and she felt I could offer her viewers information they would find useful. Second, I now had footage to show her what I was like on television.

I was interviewed by Pat Robertson on *The 700 Club* in March 2010. They flew me to their location in Virginia Beach. It was really neat to meet and talk with Pat Robertson. What was especially exciting for me was how I had come full circle. As a baby, I had been very sick with spinal meningitis. After giving me medicine, the doctors told my parents they had done all they could, and my life was in God's hands now. My family called *The 700 Club* and they prayed for me on the show. Now, 34 years later, my name was mentioned again, but as part of a much happier occasion.

The next month Clark Howard visited my school and interviewed Tracy, Ava and me for his television show. Clark is the host of the nationally syndicated consumer advocate radio show *The Clark Howard Show* as well as an author himself and host of his own television show on HLN. I had listened to Clark's radio show for years and enjoyed watching him on television.

It was so nice of him (and his crew) to make the journey to my school. Actually, I had emailed his producer by mistake; I thought I was emailing another producer of a completely different show. But I got an immediate response and since I'm not too far away from Atlanta, where their studio is, they decided to shoot numerous clips at my school. I think this one was destined to be. I guess it shows that you never know what doors might open when you ask.

Clark talked with some of the young students about managing money and answered questions from some of the teachers. It was informative and entertaining for all of us. I especially enjoyed his interview with my family and me. I knew he was pretty frugal himself so I think we were right up his alley.

In February 2011, Tracy, Ava, Ella and I were interviewed by Christine Romans for her television show *Your Bottom Line*. This was one of my favorite interviews because Tracy was recognized on national TV for all that she does. As you'll learn reading this book, our family's success with money is due in large part to Tracy. I'm the money strategist in our marriage but she runs our household and makes it all work.

In March 2011, I was invited to appear on the television show *Today with Marilyn and Sarah*. This is a Christian-based show run by Marilyn Hickey Ministries. They flew me out to their headquarters near Denver, Colorado, and taped me for two of their shows. It was a wonderful experience. *Today with Marilyn and Sarah* airs worldwide and I was told that these shows could reach over 1 billion viewers!

New Book, with Another Simple Message

Although my first book exceeded my expectations on the attention it received, I felt I could do a better job in helping more people and so I decided to write another book. *How to Survive (and Perhaps Thrive) on a Teacher's Salary* is good, but the intended audience was obviously teachers. I knew the advice I gave could benefit many others.

It's been six years since I wrote *How to Survive*. We now have two children and Tracy has been able to remain at home raising them. I'm still in the classroom teaching special needs students. Even though we've been living off my teaching salary alone, we have no debt except our mortgage, have continued to invest each month for our retirement and our children's college, have an emergency fund in place and basically live a "wealthy" life on a moderate income.

A Simple Book of Financial Wisdom: Teach Yourself (and Your Kids) How to Live Wealthy with Little Money provides information that can apply to just about everyone. A basic education in finances will help you become financially secure, and this simple book is the first step.

Thank you for taking some precious time out of your life to read this book. Connect with me:

Facebook.com/SimpleFinancialWisdom

Twitter.com/DannyKofke

DannyKofke.blogspot.com.

~ Danny

CHAPTER 1
Why Are We Broke?

We need to *think* about money more. We need to educate ourselves about finances, our own situation, and how to plan for the future and for our families.

Take a look at these sobering statistics. Then I'll share some celebrity money stories to help me prove a point.

• According to the *Wall Street Journal*, nearly 70% of consumers live paycheck to paycheck.

This is one of the main reasons that so many people are in trouble. When you're living paycheck to paycheck and something unexpected happens—you lose your job, your car needs new brakes, you get a big dentist bill—you are immediately in financial distress.

• According to a Marist Institute poll, 55% of Americans "always" or "sometimes" worry about money.

Well, this is interesting. According to the *Wall Street Journal* stat, 70% of consumers live paycheck to paycheck, yet the Marist Institute poll says that only 55% of them worry about money. I guess the other 15% aren't paying attention.

- In 1929, only 2% of the homes in America had a mortgage against them. By 1962, only 2% did not have a mortgage against them.

The American Dream has become a nightmare for many.

- According to *USA Today*, due to an insufficient amount of savings, 60% of the 77 million baby boomers will not have the means to support their current standard of living when they reach retirement age.

Wow! This is why it's so important to start preparing for your retirement as soon as possible. You'll have worked for many years by the time you reach retirement age. Start investing and saving while you're young so that your "golden years" can be everything you imagine.

- According to a 2008 survey by the National Foundation for Credit Counseling, 76 million adults say they don't have any non-retirement savings. Of those who do have a cash fund, 61% don't have enough to cover three months of income.

An emergency fund is so important. It gives you a sense of freedom and can turn a potential catastrophe into an inconvenience instead.

- According to the New York Life Insurance Company, the first group of 78.1 million baby boomers turns 65 in 2011. Out of this group, 40% must delay retirement to save for a preferred lifestyle and 22% have to delay retirement so that they can afford basic expenses.

This means that more than 6 out of 10 people cannot retire when they want to and may not ever be able to. These people will have worked for much of their lives and then find that they have to continue to work because of poor planning.

· **A new car selling for $28,800 (the 2008 average) will lose about $17,280 of its value in the first four years, making it worth $11,520. You are losing $360 per month in value.**

This is like taking a $100 bill and throwing it out of the window of your car every week for four consecutive years.

· **According to a 2008 study done by Sallie Mae and Gallup, only 9% of families use college savings funds such as 529 plans.**

We Americans will pay for our little girls to go to the best dance classes when they are four and sign our boys up for private baseball instruction when they are six but don't put away any money for their college years.

· **28% of Americans spent more time watching reality TV last month than they spent planning and preparing for retirement over the past 10 years!**

We invest our time watching "real" housewives or someone and her eight kids but don't invest in ourselves.

Celebrity Money Stories

Let's play a little game called "Name that Celebrity's Financial Story." I'll give you the background—see if you know who it is.

———— · ————

This person was a boxing champion and holds the record as the youngest boxer to win the WBC, WBA and IBF world heavyweight titles. In fact, he was the first heavyweight to hold these three titles simultaneously. He's one of the best heavyweight boxers of all time and is ranked number 16 on *Ring* magazine's list of the 100 greatest punchers.

One of his nicknames was "the Baddest Man on the Planet." He won his first 19 professional fights by knockout and 12 of these knockouts came in the first round. He unified the belts in the heavyweight division and became the undisputed heavyweight champion of the world in the late 1980s.

Despite receiving over $30 million for several of his fights and earning over $300 million during his boxing career he declared bankruptcy in 2003.

Who is this celebrity? Mike Tyson.

— • —

This actress appeared in hundreds of ads throughout the early 1970s. In 1976, after a successful five-year career as a model, she moved to Los Angeles to become an actress. She had guest roles on shows such as *Starsky and Hutch* and *Charlie's Angels*. She had her breakout role in 1983 as a Bond girl in the film *Never Say Never Again*, starring opposite Sean Connery. This led to a role in 1984's *The Natural* opposite Robert Redford in which she was nominated for a Golden Globe award as best supporting actress. She played Vicki Vale in the 1989 film *Batman*.

Despite such success, this actress made some costly financial mistakes—including buying the city of Braselton, Georgia (which, as it happens, is located five minutes from my house)—and was forced to declare bankruptcy.

Who is this actress? Kim Basinger.

— • —

Next on the list is an R&B singer, songwriter and actress. She has won six Grammy awards and sold over 40 million records.

This singer topped the Billboard chart in 1993 with her self-titled debut album. She followed this up with another album entitled *Secrets* that contained the number-one hit songs "You're Makin' Me High" and "Unbreak My Heart." Despite the success of these two albums, she filed for bankruptcy.

Not long after, she bounced back with another chart-topping album, *The Heat.* In 2009, she released the album *Pulse* which spawned the popular R&B hit "Yesterday." She also starred on the seventh season of the hit reality show *Dancing with the Stars.*

Despite fresh success after her initial financial problems, this performer didn't learn her lesson; in October 2010 she once again filed for bankruptcy.

Who is this Grammy winner? Toni Braxton.

——— • ———

Here's another performer. This person is a rapper, entertainer, business entrepreneur, dancer and actor. He is known for his hit songs (including the wildly popular "U Can't Touch This"), dance style and his trademark pants. He's sold more than 50 million records and was a household name and pop icon.

This person is considered an innovator of pop rap and is the first hip hop artist to achieve diamond status for an album. In addition, BET ranked him as the seventh best dancer of all time and *Vibe* declared him the 17th favorite rapper.

Despite such success, this person went $13 million in debt and eventually filed for bankruptcy in 1996. He sold his mansion for a fraction of what he paid for it and later said, "My priorities should have always been God, family, community and then business. Instead they had been business, business and business."

In 1997, he was the subject of an episode of the *Oprah Winfrey Show*. He admitted that he had already used up most of his fortune of over $20 million, and went on to say that money is nothing if it doesn't bring peace and if priorities are wrong.

Who is this rapper/entertainer? M.C. Hammer.

———— • ————

Our next celebrity was a recording artist, dancer, songwriter and singer. Commonly referred to as the King of Pop, he's recognized as the most successful entertainer of all time by Guinness World Records.

His songs include "Beat It," "Billie Jean," "Black or White," "Scream" and "Thriller." His *Thriller* is the best-selling album of all time. His other albums, including *Off the Wall, Bad, Dangerous* and *HIStory* are also among the best-selling albums of all time.

He is one of the few artists to have been inducted into the Rock and Roll Hall of Fame twice. He won 13 Grammy awards, 26 American Music awards, had 13 number-one songs and was estimated to have sold over 750 million records.

His total lifetime earnings from royalties on his recordings and videos, along with revenue from concerts and endorsements, have been estimated at $500 million. Even so, there were estimates that he was over $400 million in debt at the time of his death in 2009.

I'm sure you know who this is but, for the record, it is Michael Jackson.

———— • ————

Our last celebrity is a well-known movie actor. Some of his memorable roles include Bo "Bandit" Darville in *Smokey and the Bandit*, Lewis Medlock in *Deliverance*, Bobby "Gator" McCluskey in *White Lightning*, J.J. McClure in *The Cannonball Run* and Jack Horner in *Boogie Nights*. He has starred in over 90 films and 300 television episodes.

Despite a lot of success, this star's finances were in very bad shape because of an extravagant lifestyle, a costly divorce and failed investments in some restaurant chains. He filed for bankruptcy in 1996 with $6.6 million in assets and $11.2 million in debts. He even had to resort to selling his legendary mustache at auction to help pay his bills.

Who is this former college football player? Burt Reynolds.

───── • ─────

We may know all about Snookie and "the Situation" or who's on *Dancing with the Stars,* but many of us don't know how much we have in our Roth IRA—or for that matter know what a Roth IRA is.

Let these statistics and stories be a wake-up call. The need for a financial education is clear. Don't be broke.

CHAPTER 2
Learning by Example

Many of our parents and grandparents told us we needed to save for rainy days, but most of us believed the storm wouldn't be too bad. People in my generation—I am 35—have never experienced bad financial times like our grandparents might have during the Great Depression; however, in 2008, many of us realized that we didn't have a large enough umbrella and could do nothing when the rains came.

Consider for a moment those who went through the Great Depression. In its aftermath, they typically didn't end up driving a Rolls-Royce or living in a 4,000-square-foot house but many people from this generation have enough money saved to cover their living expenses for a while. You see, they lived through some very difficult times. Many know what it's like to stand in line for food or not being able to provide for their families.

Today, unfortunately, there are plenty of folks who are having a hard time paying their electric bill or buying groceries. How painful, and how scary, especially for those with families.

If poor spending habits put you in a bad situation, my hope is that you will learn from your past and never allow yourself to get in this situation again. It can be very difficult to make a change (which is why most New Year's resolutions are broken by February) and change is usually uncomfortable—especially when it's good for us. It might be hard to put money into your savings account rather than buy the newest iPhone, but think how soundly you will sleep knowing you have money in the bank in case something unexpected happens.

—— *The American Dream: A Fictional Story* ——

Jim and Laura are a typical American couple. They just got married last year after dating for four years. Jim is a manager of a local department store and Laura is a school-teacher. They make a combined salary of $100,000 a year, and look forward to raises and increased incomes in their future. They have around $3,000 in their savings account—which seems ample since they are certain they'll continue to make more money each year—and both drive new cars. They also go shopping whenever they want and pretty much buy anything they like without thinking twice. In addition, they eat out most nights of the week but try to keep it cheap; they usually don't spend more than $30 for these dinners.

After renting an apartment for six months, they decide it's time to buy a house. Even though it's just the two of them right now, they want at least a 2,000-square-foot house because children are on the horizon. Jim and Laura find the "perfect" house but it's a little above the amount they wanted to spend. Their Realtor® tells them that it's not a problem. They can sign up for a five-year adjustable rate mortgage (ARM) and by the time it adjusts, they'll have so much equity in their house they can just refinance. The housing market is strong and they're confi-dent their home will go up in value considering the prime neighborhood it's in.

Both Jim's and Laura's parents live in much smaller

homes but, after some talk, the couple feels they deserve this larger house because they work so hard and all their married friends are getting big houses too. Jim and Laura sign on the dotted line and their American Dream begins.

Fast-forward five years. Jim and Laura are now the proud parents of a little boy, James, and a girl, Sarah. After having James, Laura took eight weeks off from teaching to stay home and loved every minute of it. She wanted to stay home longer but they went through their savings on that 10-day Caribbean cruise before she got pregnant. She began to feel very upset at having to send James to daycare but there was no way around it—they needed her check to pay the bills.

Jim saw how unhappy she was and one night decided to have a talk. It was very encouraging and they both agreed to make a change and start saving so Laura could eventually stay home. This change lasted a few months before they started spending their entire paychecks again on things such as new clothes and dinners out.

Last year Laura had Sarah and was only able to stay home with her for four weeks before having to return to work. She now spends over half of her take-home pay on daycare expenses. Laura dreads going to work and hits the snooze button at least five times every morning because she hates getting up to face another day.

Jim is not doing much better. He's had to lay off most of his salespeople. The raise he was promised every year did not happen. There are even rumors that his job might be the next to go. He's started to look for other jobs but nobody seems to be hiring in his area of expertise.

To make a bad situation even worse, Jim and Laura's five-year ARM is scheduled to adjust this year and their monthly mortgage payment will increase by $500. The house has dropped greatly in value and Jim and Laura are underwater on their loan so they cannot refinance.

In addition, after James was born, Jim and Laura

began to use their credit cards again with the promise of paying them off in full each month. That plan didn't pan out and they now have $10,000 in credit card debt. They both have a lot of trouble falling asleep at night and don't feel optimistic about either their marriage or their future. They have started arguing more and more—something they never did in the good old days—and these arguments usually concern their finances. What was supposed to have been their American Dream has turned into a scary nightmare!

—— • ——

Not a pretty picture, is it? I hope your story is not like Jim and Laura's but, unfortunately, I know a lot of people can relate to this couple. The great news for Jim and Laura (and maybe you too) is that life allows us to learn and adapt and change.

In the previous chapter you read about celebrities earning lots and losing everything. And you've just read this fictional story of Jim and Laura. They're obviously examples *not* to follow—but we can learn so much from them.

Many people don't see the need to learn about money and how to manage it correctly. They bury their heads in the sand and don't want to be worried about the true state of their finances because, if they did, they might have to change their spending habits. The thing is, if you continue to make poor financial decisions, these actions will eventually come back to haunt you. Think about those celebrities in Chapter 1. They made a lot of money but still found themselves in trouble. If you make $5 million a year but spend $6 million, you'll wake up one day and find that you are broke.

The great news is that it doesn't have to be this way. We

can educate ourselves, find examples to emulate, create goals and take action. In Chapters 4 and 5 I'll describe my family's self-taught financial education. But before that, in the next chapter, let's ask ourselves: does money even make us happy?

DANNY KOFKE

CHAPTER 3
Does Money Make Us Happy?

The basic fact is that if you spend more than you earn, you'll eventually be in trouble. It doesn't matter if you make $10,000, $100,000 or even $1,000,000 a year; the same principle applies.

Why do so many of us spend money we don't have? I feel this is because we are emotionally insecure. We live in one of the wealthiest nations on Earth, yet so many people are unhappy. A lot of us seek professional help for this very reason. Clearly, having money can take away many worries, but it doesn't automatically guarantee happiness.

Think about some of your peers. Do any of them make a lot of money but have nothing to show for it? There might be some who press the snooze button numerous times on Monday morning because they dread going to work. Even if you make $500,000 a year, if you are unhappy Monday through Friday I don't feel you are "wealthy." Many of these same people spend money and buy things to make themselves "happy." Once the weekend rolls around, they can come up with some great reasons to buy things. "I work so hard and put up with so much I deserve_____." Fill in this blank with clothes, jewelry, eating out, and so on. So many people do this in search of happiness.

Let's face it, buying things can bring about a sense of joy. But only for a moment. If I go out and buy a shirt it feels great. The first few times I wear it, it feels good. Then, after five or six times of wearing this shirt, something happens—it becomes old. How many of us have looked in our closet and said, "I have nothing to wear" even though we have 50 outfits staring back at us? At one point in time we liked these clothes (or at least we liked them enough to buy them) but, after a while, that feeling goes away. If we base our feelings of happiness on materialistic things, we will be in a constant cycle of having to buy things to make ourselves feel happy.

I feel that money problems are 80% emotional. Many people know not to buy things they cannot afford using credit cards but they still do it. Let's say we use a credit card with a 24% annual percentage rate (APR) and buy something that costs $100. Then we don't make a single payment on this bill the entire year. How much would we owe? If you said $124, you're right: 24% of $100 = $24; $100 + $24 = $124. The math is pretty easy but many folks still buy things they don't have the money for. This is where the emotions come into play.

A lot of people are unhappy in their lives—be it spiritually, in their careers, with their spouse, and so on. To combat this unhappiness they buy things. I think that money and weight problems often go hand-in-hand. We now have easy access to pretty much all of the nutritional information of the food we eat, yet nearly two-thirds of our country is overweight or even obese.

We know how bad it is to continually stop by our favorite fast-food restaurant to order a number 3 and super-size it, but many still do. Why do we do this to ourselves? I feel the answer is the same as why we buy things we can't afford—it gives us a temporary feeling of satisfaction. I know this doesn't apply to everyone but I feel this is a main reason that our nation has become so overweight and in debt.

It's pretty simple to have money and be skinny on paper. If you lived by the phrase "Eat Less Than You Burn, Spend Less Than You Earn" (what a great idea for a t-shirt!), you would most likely be thin and have money. It sounds so simple, but it can get complicated when the emotions get involved.

A Happiness Study

According to a 2009 study focusing on 450,000 Americans and how they evaluate their happiness, a yearly salary of $75,000 is the number after which people's day-to-day happiness no longer improves. This study was conducted by psychologist Daniel Kahneman and economist Angus Deaton.

This tells us that as people earn more money, their day-to-day happiness rises until they hit $75,000. After that it's just more stuff, with no gain in happiness.

It doesn't mean the wealthy and ultra-wealthy are equally happy. Having more money does boost people's life assessment all the way up the income ladder. People who earned $180,000 a year reported more overall satisfaction than people earning $100,000.

But, according to Kahneman and Deaton's study, someone making $375,000 a year will not be happier on a day-to-day basis than someone with an annual salary of $75,000 though they will probably feel they have a better overall life.

After reading this study I was intrigued. I knew that teaching ranked among the most satisfying jobs and I wanted to see what other careers ranked high in overall contentment and what their average salaries were. Here is a list of the top 10 most satisfying careers with their average annual salary:

10	Operating Engineer	$67,200
9	Financial Advisor/Planner	$62,385
8	Psychologist	$78,967
7	Artist	$51,378
6	Education Administrator	$66,061
5	Teacher	$41,193
4	Author	$51,907
3	Physical Therapist	$66,628
2	Firefighter	$44,504
1	Clergyman	$53,200

I must say that unless you write a love story about vampires the author's salary might be high but, all joking aside, I find this list to be very interesting. Only one of these careers averages above that magical $75,000 annual figure, yet many people in these professions are very satisfied and content in their chosen paths. Why is this so?

Many of these careers are a calling. The people who have jobs in these fields usually got into them because they are passionate about what they do first and foremost. These days it's hard to complain about low pay since so many are struggling right now and would love a bigger paycheck, but I think most would agree that a firefighter has to have a passion for rescuing others, willingly risking his/her life, and isn't doing this just for the $44,000 a year he/she makes. When you have a job that you feel is your calling, you don't need to make a large salary to feel content with it.

⸺ *Change Your Perspective* ⸺

Before you begin reading the next chapter and start on the path to managing your money better, I want you to change your perspective. Many of us have a lot but never take the time to truly appreciate all we have. It's become a cultural habit to constantly look ahead and strive for more.

Don't get me wrong, I think America is the greatest country on Earth. We have some of the strongest work ethics around. In our wonderful country, you can achieve great success through ambition and hard work. However, problems arise when some folks are so focused on accumulating more that they never take the time to relish what they have accomplished and/or all they have.

Life in Poland

I was very fortunate to have the opportunity to live in another country. Shortly after getting married, Tracy and I moved to Krakow, Poland, to teach at the American International School of Krakow. It was great to spend our first two years of marriage in Europe—it was almost like a two-year honeymoon. We traveled to 10 countries and got to have some really neat experiences. But the best part about living in Poland was that it changed our perspective.

Our first place together was a small one-bedroom apartment. Now, coming from the land of 2,000-square-foot "starter" homes, this apartment seemed *really* small to us. The building we lived in was in the middle of the city and we were surrounded by Polish families. Some of these families had five people living in apartments the same size as our own.

We had a hard time believing this at first. I mean, how could this be possible? After our initial shock began to fade, we started to see that our neighbors were more content and happier than some of our friends back home who had much larger places to live and much more "stuff." This got us thinking. Maybe, just maybe, buying big houses and other items doesn't automatically lead to happiness.

Teaching Special Needs Students

For the past five years I've taught what is known here in Georgia as a severe/profound special needs class. Many of the students have IQs below 30, some are in wheelchairs, some are fed using a feeding tube and most use nonverbal cues to communicate. A lot of people have told me that I must have a big heart and great patience to teach these students, but the truth is that I feel like I'm the lucky one; these students actually teach me more than I could ever give them. They get joy out of what many of us take for granted.

I had one student who was happy as he could be when he was eating marshmallows out of Lucky Charms cereal. I teach a little girl who smiles the biggest and prettiest smile I've ever seen when she sees Blue from *Blue's Clues*. In these days of consumption and wanting more, I get reminded on a daily basis of the little things that most of us can find happiness in but overlook in the pursuit of wanting more.

A Conversation I Will Never Forget

I live approximately one hour outside of Atlanta. Sometimes when I'm going to appear on a national television show, the station will send a driver to take me to the studio and bring me back home. I once had a driver named Soulley and we had a memorable conversation.

During our drive, we talked about our lives and he told me about growing up in Senegal, a country in western

Africa, and about coming to America. He grew up without many things and said his entire village pretty much shared all they had. According to Soulley, 90% of his community wanted to come and live in the States. I asked why and he said it was because of the freedom to do and be almost anything you want to.

I will never forget what Soulley told me next. He said that even if one has a low-paying job here in America, he/she can still afford to have a place of his/her own and a small television set to watch shows on. I had never really thought of it in these terms before. I know it's all relative, but we Americans think it's a tragedy when our iPhones don't get a signal. There are so many living in other countries who don't have electricity or running water. Sometimes it takes someone with a completely different point-of-view to help us see things in a different light.

I used to live in Florida. In September 2004, our city was directly hit by two hurricanes within a span of 24 days. There was a lot of damage to our house—we needed a new roof and our back porch was destroyed, among other things—and we were without electricity for a while.

Now, September in South Florida is not the best time of year to be without power. My brother lent us a generator which was helpful, but it wasn't fun to have to fill it with gasoline every few hours. I still remember when our power was restored. This was like the greatest gift from God. I also remember thinking about how many people go without electricity all the time, and how soon I would take it for granted.

Sure enough, less than one week later, my main concern was getting the satellite to work so I could watch football. I didn't even think twice about how nice it was to have power again—I became accustomed to it. I guess what I want to point out is that most of us are very blessed but, because we are so used to having certain things, we tend to overlook how fortunate we are and how much we do have.

I know that how we view money and our lives is all relative to our experiences. What one person considers to be a success might be a disappointment to another. For example, just a few weeks ago I ran a 5K race in under 29 minutes and was pleased with my performance. However, someone that had trained longer and harder than I might be disappointed with this time. Before you begin to make a change in your life, I think it's important to take a look at how you view things.

One way we do this in my family is to eat dinner together almost every night. I feel this is important for many reasons but one of the things we usually discuss is something good that happened to each of us that day. For my daughter Ella, it might be how she had fun blowing bubbles or the good time she had playing with a friend. I might share that someone gave me a compliment or how beautiful the weather was—things that I might otherwise overlook if not for this conversation. The important thing is that we recognize those blessings—no matter how large or small—that we have in our lives.

Another way to change your perspective is to make goals for yourself and write them down. It's so easy to focus on our shortcomings and what we cannot do or have. Making a list of achievable goals gives us a sense of empowerment.

For example, let's say I want to run a 10K race. I probably wouldn't be able to just step out my front door and run 6.2 miles without any training. Instead, I'd come up with a jogging plan to help me reach this goal. I might run 1 mile the first week, move it up to 2 miles the next and continue increasing the amount I jog until I reach my goal of running 10 kilometers. I would be working towards a larger goal but, in the process, I would have success completing shorter goals to lead up to this bigger goal. I'd see progress on a weekly basis which would empower me to keep going.

I want you to write down some money goals you have for yourself. They can be smaller, short-term goals (*I will only eat lunch out three times this week*) and/or larger, long-term goals (*I will have $10,000 in my emergency fund by this time next year*). Post these goals somewhere you'll see them on a daily basis.

Once you achieve one of these goals, put a gold star next to it (I mean it!) or simply cross it off your list and see how good that feels. By creating goals, you are holding yourself accountable for your actions—something many people could improve upon. In addition, you're making a map of where you want to be in the future.

If I wanted to drive my car to California, I wouldn't just get behind the wheel and start driving (with my sense of direction I'd probably end up in Mexico). I would look at a map to see the direction I needed to head in. The same thing holds true with money. You need to have a destination in mind in order to get there.

CHAPTER 4
A Financial Primer: The Basics of Money

People get into financial trouble when they don't know how they're spending their money. Living in a house you can't afford and driving a car that's too expensive will obviously get you into trouble, but for many, it's those day-to-day expenses that add up fast over time.

For example, let's say you eat lunch out every workday, Monday through Friday. You're being frugal, you feel, since you get by for $5 a day. You probably don't think twice about spending $5—it's not a large amount, after all. What you may not realize, however, is how this can, over time, add up to some serious change. $5 each workday adds up to $25 a week. Spending $25 each week adds up to $1,300 a year! I hope the lunches were good.

⸺ *Your Major Expenses* ⸺

Many people have no idea what their major expenses are and what they spend on them. They just write a check or pay their bills online without thinking twice about where this money is going. Let's change that.

Here's a list of the major expenses that many of us have. I want you to take the time to write down how much you spend on each of these expenses on a monthly basis.

If a certain item doesn't apply to you, just skip over it.

Savings
Retirement fund $ _____

College fund $ _____

Housing
Mortgage/rent $ _____

Property taxes $ _____

Homeowners insurance $ _____

Federal/state income taxes $ _____

Transportation
Car payment $ _____

Car insurance $ _____

Fuel $ _____

Utilities
Electricity $ _____

Water $ _____

Phone—home and cell $ _____

Internet $ _____

Cable/satellite $ _____

Garbage $ _____

Medical/Health
Life insurance $ _____

Disability insurance $ _____

Health insurance $ _____

Personal/Daily Living
Student loan $ _____

Credit card(s) $ _____

Food (grocery store, eating out) $ _____

Entertainment $ _____

Contributions $ _____

One thing Tracy and I do that helps us keep track of our major expenses is we write them down on a Post-it note that stays in our checkbook. We write down the day of the month that this expense is paid, the expense and the amount. Here's an example:

1st	Mortgage	$1,000
5th	Roth IRA	$150
10th	Satellite	$75
12th	Phone/internet	$80
20th	Life insurance	$25
25th	Electric bill	$140 (avg.)
25th	Water	$30 (avg.)

This allows us to see what bills still need to be paid on any given day. For example, if it's October 15th, I can look in our checkbook and know we still have to pay for our life insurance, our electric bill and our water bill. This helps us greatly in keeping on top of our money.

Another thing we do is deduct our expenses before we spend our money. Let's say our monthly bills are the same amounts listed above. If you add these up you get a total of $1,500 in major monthly expenses. I get paid a set amount on the last day of each month. We'll say my monthly take-home pay is $2,500. We would subtract $1,500 (our monthly expenses) from $2,500 (my take-home pay) to get $1,000. In this example, we'd have $1,000 left for the month to cover our other expenses.

We then take that $1,000 and divide it by 4—the number of weeks in a typical month (if the month happens to have 5 weeks we would divide the $1,000 by 5)—to get $250. We then know that we have that amount to spend each week. This is an easy way for us to stay within our budget.

Track Your Spending

Congratulations, you know more about how you're spending your money than many of your friends. Now that you know where a majority of your cash is going, let's create a spending plan to see how the rest is being spent.

But first, I must warn you that this will not be easy. You might want to curse me out while you're doing this, but I promise it will help and will probably even save you some money—so let's get to it!

You are going to track your spending for one month. I want you to carry a pen and piece of paper with you at all times and write down everything and anything you spend money on. I know some people prefer an electronic device but I think pen and paper is better because you don't have to worry about something not working. In addition, the information written down is in your very own hand-writing so the emotional (there's that word again) attachment will be greater.

Once the month is up, sit down and analyze this list to see how you spent your money. The greatest thing about this approach is that the numbers don't lie—you wrote them down yourself. You'll now be able to see ways in which you can cut back. Many of us spend money on things we truly don't need. If you happen to have the money to buy whatever you want, that's great, but you're the exception. Most of us would like to add a little more to our monthly income.

There are three ways you can make more money each month: get a higher-paying job, get a second job or cut back on your spending. Let's face it, although it *is* possible to get a higher-paying job, it's more difficult than it was five years ago. Getting a second job is also possible, but that means more time away from the family. That leaves us with Plan C—changing some of the ways we spend money.

By tracking what you buy, you can cut back in areas that might not be so important. You might not miss $10 here or $20 there but remember, this can add up fast. Seeing where your money is going, on paper, is pretty powerful.

Tracking your spending also gives you some options. You might realize that you ate dinner out four times this month and also went to the movies twice. If you're looking to add money to your bank account, you now see where it can come from—you can stop going out to dinner or cut back on theater tickets.

What if these things are too important for you to give up? Well, you can now look over the other ways you spent money and eliminate some of these. You'll see that tracking your spending gives you options that you otherwise would not have.

I must admit that I, like most people, want "things." And it doesn't help matters that Madison Avenue spends billions of dollars each year to get us to spend our money. According to *American Demographics* magazine, the average young person will be exposed to 23 million advertising impressions before he/she is 21 years old! With that much exposure it's amazing that more people aren't in debt.

If I see someone pull up next to me in a shiny new BMW, of course I want it! The thing is, I *can* have it—but something will have to give. I'll either have to get a higher-paying job or go out and get a second job, which means I won't see much of my family. Or Tracy will have to go back to work.

Every action has a consequence. I think too many of us don't take this into account. We're a society of "I see it, I want it, I buy it," without thinking about the future ramifications of these kinds of decisions. You can have almost anything you desire, but everything comes with a price—and everything has to be paid for.

Reacquaint Yourself with George, Abraham, and Andrew

To take your spending plan a little further, you might want to use a cash-only spending plan. This does require some discipline but can help you greatly.

Once you know how much you need on a weekly basis, pull that exact amount out for your weekly spending money. A word of caution before you begin: you might have to play with this number for a few weeks before you have it down. Don't become discouraged if your number is off the first couple of weeks—readjust as needed and stick with it.

Let's say after tracking your spending you see that you need $300 each week for things such as food, gas and any other expenses that come up. Select one day each week that you go to your local ATM machine and pull this exact amount out. This will be your spending money to last the entire week.

For this example, you decide to take your weekly spending money out every Friday. You are doing well but both cars needed gas this week and by Thursday you have no money left. Your friends call and want to go out for dinner. This is where it gets hard. You'll have to risk sounding weird (I mean, isn't it weird to not spend money you don't have?) and tell them no thanks. You can take a rain check but won't be able to spend more money until Friday rolls around again.

There are many advantages to using a cash-only system. We have to go back to your emotions again. Many people have an emotional attachment to those crisp green bills. We know how much sweat went into earning those dollars which makes them much harder to part with compared to swiping a piece of plastic through a machine. In fact, there are studies that show you will spend 12–18% less when using cash compared to plastic. Go ahead and try it for yourself. Most people think twice before parting with cash which is a step in the right direction.

Another advantage to using cash is the time you'll save. I've talked to some folks who tell me their lives are so hectic that they don't have the time to balance their checkbooks. They end up with overdraft fees and are definitely not in control of their money. Making one withdrawal a week can save you time since there's just one transaction to keep track of and write down. (If you don't have 30 seconds in your week to write down this single transaction, you are reading the wrong book.)

In addition, you can save money using cash. We've all heard how tough times are for some stores. If you use cash, you can take advantage of this. Many stores are willing to give a discount if you pay with dollar bills. I had a friend who was in the market for a television set with a retail price of $1,000. I told her to walk into the store with $700 cash and see what would happen. After a few minutes of negotiating, she got this set for the $700 she walked in with. It never hurts to ask. The worst the salesperson can tell you is no.

⸺ *Save Some Money* ⸺

Ready to start "earning" more money by cutting back on your spending? Here are some ways you can start saving today.

Cook at Home

If both the husband and wife work, this might be difficult, especially at first. Start out with the habit of cooking at home once a week and slowly increase the frequency until you find a balance between saving money and getting stressed out.

Make a List Before Going Shopping

It's called impulse buying for a reason. Humans simply have a tough time resisting the temptation to purchase extras while shopping. Without a list you will buy items that you simply do not need. Grocery stores are masterful at placing tempting items at the ends of aisles to get your attention.

Even worse is when you forget to purchase the actual item you went to the store for in the first place. If you're cooking at home, pre-plan a rough menu and make a list before going grocery shopping. Getting all the food you need in one trip can help you avoid another unnecessary trip and the temptations that go along with that.

Make Your Own Halloween Costumes

Tracy has made our daughter's costumes the past few years. One year, she made a skeleton costume that looked identical to one that was for sale in a Pottery Barn catalog for $60. This homemade costume saved us $50! Tracy has also made butterfly and salt-and-pepper costumes. These costumes were adorable and you would have thought we bought them from a specialty store.

Get a New Cell Phone Plan

This might not apply to everyone, but we use our cell phones very little. My school is three miles away from home so I don't have a long commute and don't need to use a cell phone that much. A few years ago, we had a plan in which we were paying $50 per month for a cell phone that we barely used. We now have prepaid cells and average about $20 per month on both of these combined.

I've talked to people who tell me they have no money but tote around the newest iPhone. These people *do* have money but are choosing to spend it on items they may not really need. I know that some folks need to have constant access to others, but if you're serious about getting out of debt, you might have to cut back some in this area.

Use Your Local Library

We all know the library is a great place to get books for free, but a lot of people don't realize that many libraries also have CDs and DVDs available for checkout. Most libraries offer great free programs for all ages. At our local library, my family has watched movies and seen a juggler, a magician and tap dancers. These were fun family events that only cost us the gas to get there.

Ask for Free Stuff

This may surprise you, but we subscribe to the NFL Sunday Ticket on satellite TV. This is one splurge that is important to us; we have family time watching football together on Sundays. A few years ago, I saw an ad in a sports magazine saying that new subscribers to this service would receive an added feature worth $99 for free.

I called my satellite company and said that I already subscribed and wanted this free add-on service. After 15 minutes of being put on hold, my mission was accomplished.

Remember, it never hurts to ask—the worst that can happen is that you're told no and are back in the same situation you were in before asking.

Save a Little Every Day

Some people buy their coffee on the way to work. This practice can add up easily to over $100 per month. If you made your own coffee at home, you could save up to $25 a week, which adds up to $1,300 a year!

Another way to save is to bring your lunch to work. On average, you'll spend at least $5 eating a fast-food lunch and even more for a sit-down restaurant meal. This adds up quickly.

You can also save money by purchasing sodas at the store rather than from a vending machine. Some machines charge $1.00 per soda, and I've even seen some priced as high as $1.75. I wait until there's a sale at the grocery store and buy four 12-packs for $12. If you had one soda a day while at work, this would save you almost $200 a year!

A final way to save is to drink water from your tap. According to the Container Recycling Institute, Americans buy 25 billion single-serve plastic water bottles a year. If this includes you and/or your family, you're spending a lot of money on something that you can pretty much get for free. The Earth Policy Institute estimates that the average family of four spends around $1,095 per person every year on bottled water—that's a whopping total of $4,380!

Use Coupons at the Grocery Store

Tracy really got serious about using coupons in 2010 and the results were great—we saved over $1,600 that year by using coupons and shopping for deals. (Later in this chapter, we'll talk about this at more length.)

For most people, it's not how much you make, but how well you plan your spending. Try some or all of these tips; they'll help you on your journey towards financial success.

—— *Work with Your Family as a Team* ——

I feel that my family's success is due in large part to how Tracy and I work together as a team. We set goals for our family and strive to achieve them with each other's support.

It's extremely important for a husband and wife to be on the same page with their finances. Here are a few statistics that demonstrate this:

According to a survey by ForbesWoman and the

National Endowment for Financial Education, 31% of people lied to their spouses about money, 67% argued over money lies and 16% of these money lies led to divorce.

A Utah State study showed that a couple with $10,000 in debt and no savings is about twice as likely to divorce as a couple with $10,000 in savings and no credit card debt.

A study done by Citibank found that 57% of divorced couples said money fights were the primary reason they did not get along.

I know how crazy and hectic life can be sometimes. Between kids, work and staying on top of our bills, Tracy and I are pretty busy—as are most folks. I couldn't imagine adding money troubles/arguments to the equation. I see why financial problems can lead to divorce; for many it's the straw that breaks the camel's back.

Even though I'm the numbers person in my marriage, my family would not be in good financial shape without Tracy. I asked her to contribute some of her experiences so you can see how important it is for couples to be on the same page.

⸺ *Tracy's Perspective: In Her Words* ⸺

I cannot say I have always been good with money. I've had my own evolution and it is a path that I am extremely proud of. The ironic part of my journey is that I am now more conscious of money than Danny is.

When Danny and I met, I was working on paying off the debt I had accumulated during my first years of making "real" money. I had been a teacher for four years and enjoyed my newfound freedom, eating out, having fun and living on my own. I had a car payment, student loans and some $5,000 in credit card debt.

Isn't it interesting that even though I went from earning and basically living on nothing in college to making over $30,000 a year, I still got into debt? I was, like many, on the fast track to living a life that was full of bills that I couldn't afford to pay. So I moved back to my hometown and into my old bedroom at home. This was very humbling but was worth the end result. I was grateful for the opportunity to have a fresh start.

After Danny and I grew closer and more serious, we started planning. We began keeping track of how we spent our money and discussed our short- and long-term goals. I continued living at home that year as we planned our wedding (paid for mostly by us) and continued to work on paying off my debt.

Since Danny and I were moving overseas for our first two years of marriage, we didn't have to immediately begin saving for a family or a house. We did, however, start planning for paying off our wedding expenses and then for that house and family down the road. We knew where every dollar we earned went.

In many of the conversations I've had about money with other people, I've come to a couple of conclusions that form the basis of our success. We know how much our monthly expenses are and we know how we spend our money. I have made being "cheap" kind of a game—in fact, I was frugal before being frugal was cool. As a stay-at-home mom, the way I "earn" money is by cutting back on what I spend. Every time I save a dollar it's the same as if I earned this same dollar.

I carry the checkbook with me everywhere. We did evolve from cash-only to using the debit card. We had become so accustomed to how much money we "needed" for the week that we could then trust our use of the debit card. Every time I use the card I write down the transaction in the register. I know some people save all of their receipts and then have to log it after the fact. Doing it immediately saves time and lessens the chances of forgetting or losing a receipt.

For a while, I was struggling with the balance in the register. I went to Danny and said that I needed more information. I needed to know at any given time what bills were still coming out of the balance. We came up with a Post-it stuck to the back of the register. Now, before I go to the store, I can look at the balance, quickly deduct what bills will still need to come out for the month and then divide the remaining balance with the number of weeks left in the month.

I think this is *the* biggest change we've made in the past six years. If we went over our balance we would use the credit card and then dip into savings each month to pay it off. Knowing exactly what our balance was and what it still needed to be used for practically stopped us from using our credit card and thus prevented us from going over our monthly budget. This knowledge has helped keep our savings/emergency fund full.

I've recently learned the game of couponing. I'm not as good at this as some folks I know but I did save over $1,600 last year by taking advantage of grocery store sales and using coupons. It took a little time to set this up, but shopping for deals and using coupons is something that is relatively easy to do.

I save coupons from the Sunday paper and wait for an item to go on sale. I am conscious of the sale cycle; some items go on sale regularly every six weeks. Once this happens, I can save a good chunk of change. Let's say the cereal I eat regularly costs $4 a box. One week, there's a "Buy 1, Get 1 for Free" sale on this cereal. This means that one box would cost $2. Let's say I have a 50-cents-off coupon for this item. The grocery store I shop at doubles coupons up to 50 cents, so I'd save another $1 on this box of cereal. I now got this $4 item for $1!

"Buy One, Get One" deals vary in different areas. It could mean that each item is actually 50% off or you pay full price for the one item and the other one is free. The difference is that you can use two coupons (one on each item that is 50% off) or only one if you have to pay full price. Doing this over time can lead to some serious savings.

I also cook homemade meals for my family. Not only are prepackaged foods usually less healthy than ones made from scratch, they often cost more.

Another way I cut back is the way I exercise. I jog in my neighborhood bright and early three times a week with my mother-in-law. The only cost for this is a new pair of running shoes every so often. I also check out an exercise video from our local library and work out with a friend a couple of days each week.

As with most people, there are times that I want something that's not in our budget. Danny's practical response to this is: "We can buy almost anything we desire, but you will probably have to go back to work." So far, there has never been an item, trip or other desire that has been worth giving up the life we currently live.

A friend recently commented on how happy I am. I don't live in the biggest house, drive the fanciest car or wear the most expensive jewelry. Despite not having these things, I am very content. I guess it goes to show that although having nice "stuff" can make you happy, this feeling usually doesn't last. I have loved every minute of being a stay-at-home mom and the time I've been able to devote to my family is worth way more than anything I could buy.

⟶ *The Wedding Myth* ⟶

I am extremely lucky to have found a wife like Tracy. Our goals for our family and lives are identical. We spend a lot of time planning and discussing our goals which has enabled us to be very content with what we have. We were smart to begin talking about our hopes and dreams before getting married. Many dating/engaged couples fail to do this and thus begin their marriages already in debt.

This past February I read an article in *USA Today* about Valentine's Day and weddings. Many men think about proposing on Valentine's Day thanks to various commercials showing us how magical that is. These ads show us how happy our future brides will be and how we'll live happily ever after. What these commercials don't show is this same couple ten years down the road when the realities of life (kids, bills and jobs) kick in and that special ring is not so magical anymore.

The 2008 Wedding Report shows that the average couple spends $3,215 on an engagement ring and another $2,036 on wedding bands. Add that to the $24,066 average wedding (according to www.costofwedding.com) and that comes to over $29,000 spent on a typical wedding. For most, the years you spend dating and the beginning days of being a married couple are usually some of the happiest—and when we least need to spend money. Most of us are so in love at this point we don't need anything else to make us happy. When Tracy and I moved to Poland a few months after getting married, we had no television and even did our laundry in the bathtub for the first month we were there, but we were very happy.

I know that many women have dreamed of their wedding day since they were little girls, but wouldn't this money be better utilized five years later when the kids start coming and money becomes tighter? The $5,000 spent on rings could equal 100 nights of paying a babysitter. The average $24,000 wedding could cover the cost of a cleaning lady for 10 years or 240 dinners out at $100 a pop.

I'm not saying that weddings are unimportant but expensive ones definitely don't guarantee a happy marriage. Too many people place importance on the size of an engagement ring or the type of wedding dress they're able to wear. These might be important for that one day out of your life, but they don't help a bit when the kids are keeping you up at night and you desperately need an evening out but can't afford it.

I know that this may sound unromantic. Tracy doesn't have an expensive engagement ring and although we did have a wedding, it didn't cost us nearly as much as the average wedding. Despite that, we are still deeply in love with each other almost 11 years later. And I feel that I have the best marriage one could ever dream of. In my opinion, a lifetime of happiness is worth way more than going into debt for one magical day.

CHAPTER 5
Take Control of Your Finances, Find Freedom, Plan Your Future:
Easy Steps to Follow

$\mathbf{T}$racy and I have shared with you some ways to obtain and save money. So now what should you do with it? Here are the steps that Tracy and I followed. We began them before we had children, while Tracy was working as a teacher. But anytime you start using these steps will help you get control of your finances.

⸻ *Save Money in an Emergency Fund* ⸻

It's a fact of life that rainy days will come and we'll need an umbrella. If you own a house, something will eventually need to be repaired. If you own a car, you'll need a new part if you drive it long enough. If you have children, they'll do something unexpected that will cost you money. (This reminds me of when I was 12 years old and playing kickball with my brother Kyle in our front yard. As he was heading towards home plate, I reared back and let fly the most perfect throw. There was only one little problem: Kyle decided to duck at the last second and the ball went through our bedroom window. Whoops! I'm sure my parents didn't expect that.)

I don't want to be negative—in fact, Tracy often tells me that I can be too positive. The reality is that bad things will happen and we need to be prepared. Tracy and I started our emergency fund with $2,000, which was basically one of our paychecks at that time. This wouldn't cover a major emergency but could pay for those minor, unexpected things that happen such as your air conditioning going out or needing new tires on your car. We eventually added more to this fund but started off with this amount so that we could move on to getting rid of our debt.

If you don't happen to have this amount of money sitting around, what can you do to get it? Maybe you could sell some stuff or get a second job for a while delivering newspapers early in the morning. Take another look at the tips in previous chapters. Whatever it takes, get this money ASAP. It might not be fun but remember, it's not forever.

Once you get this money, put it in a safe place where you won't impulsively spend it. Tracy and I aren't concerned about earning interest on this fund or having it grow. The purpose of this money is for emergencies only and no, a 50-inch flat-screen television set doesn't count. You should have easy access to this money and be able to get it at a moment's notice. You don't want to have it in a place where you'll be tempted to use it for non-emergencies but you also don't want it to be locked up in a CD where you might have to pay a penalty in order to have access to it. We have our emergency fund in a savings account at our local bank which works well for us.

Get Rid of Debt

Now let's figure out how you can pay off all of your debts except the mortgage (this comes later). I've given financial presentations teaching these steps and people will ask, "Doesn't it make more sense to pay off debt before starting an emergency fund?" The answer is absolutely! From a mathematical standpoint, it makes much more sense to pay off a debt with a 24% interest rate than it does earning 1% on your money in a savings account. If we're in debt, we have to remember that math probably didn't get us in this predicament. Most of us know it's not wise to buy things on credit but did so anyway.

Let's say you started this process by paying off your debt first rather than saving $2,000 in an emergency fund. You're plugging along and doing a great job; in fact, you've already paid off two credit cards. One cold winter morning you go to start your car and the battery is dead. You don't have any money so how in the world are you going to pay for this?

Yep, you guessed it, back on the credit card it goes. Many people already feel they can't handle money and here is yet another blow to their self-esteem. At this point, a lot of us might throw in the towel and revert back to our old bad spending habits.

Dave Ramsey, radio show host and author of *The Total Money Makeover*, calls this the debt snowball. Some financial experts say to pay off your debts by starting with the one that carries the highest interest rate first and go in that order. Dave, and some others, recommend starting with the debt that is the least amount. This is the approach that Tracy and I used. You begin by listing all of your debts in order from least to greatest. This includes credit card debt, medical bills and student loans. Even if the smallest debt has the lowest interest rate, pay that off first.

I know that doesn't make sense from a mathematical point-of-view but let's go back to the emotional aspect again. Many of us feel like failures when it comes to money. We list all kinds of excuses why we can't handle our finances better and thus need a game-changer. The debt snowball can definitely change the score.

Once you pay off that first debt you get a morale boost

and are motivated to keep going. Then you pay off the next debt and the momentum is rolling now. This is very similar to being on a diet. If you lose two pounds the first week you realize your hard work and effort are worth it and are motivated to lose even more. Once you get the snowball rolling it quickly becomes an avalanche.

Let's take a look at a brief example of how this works. Let's say you have a Visa credit card with a $500 balance and a 20% APR; a MasterCard with a $1,000 balance and a 16% APR; and a medical bill with a $2,000 balance and a 0% APR. Listing these debts in order looks like this:

Visa	$500	20%
MasterCard	$1,000	16%
Medical	$2,000	0%

You've been paying the minimum monthly payment on each of these debts which looks like this:

Visa	$500	20%
	$15/monthly payment	
MasterCard	$1,000	16%
	$25/monthly payment	
Medical	$2,000	0%
	$25/monthly payment *	

* There's no set minimum amount you have to pay; you've just decided to pay $25 a month towards this debt.

Now we're going to tackle the first debt, the Visa card. We'll continue to make the minimum monthly payment on the other two debts and apply extra money towards the Visa card. Let's say we come up with an extra $35 each month to add to the $15 payment we've been making.

You'll now pay $50 each month towards this debt and it will be gone in 12 months; if you continued to just make the minimum $15/month payment it would take you 50 months—over four years—to pay this off.

Now the Visa debt is gone and we have an extra $50 each month (the payment we were making on this card). We're not going to blow this "extra" money. We're going to apply this money towards the next debt, in this case the MasterCard. We've been paying the minimum $25/month towards this debt. We'll now add $50 to this amount and thus will pay $75 each month. Fast-forward 13 months and this debt will be gone. If you had continued to make the minimum $25 monthly payment you would spend 96 months (over eight years!) paying off this debt.

Okay, the credit cards are gone so we'll focus on the medical debt. We'll now be able to pay $100 each month on this debt. During the course of paying off the other two debts, we've continued to pay $25 each month towards this medical debt and now owe $1,375. Once you start paying $100 each month on this debt it too will be eliminated after 14 months.

A little over three years after beginning the debt snowball you are debt-free! What a great feeling this will be. No more late-night calls from collection agencies. You'll be able to peacefully shut your eyes at night.

See how it works? You can do this.

Tracy and I used this approach to pay off our car, and were fortunate enough to start our marriage with little debt. We met in August, got engaged in December, wed in June and then moved overseas to teach in Poland. We didn't need cars sitting around in the U.S. while we were abroad, and were able to sell both of ours. We used this money to pay for our wedding expenses.

Before leaving for Poland, we discussed how much we wanted to have when we returned home. We thought $20,000 would be a good amount for a down payment on a house, cars, furniture, and so on. We'd be starting from scratch so we needed to be prepared.

So we divided $20,000 by 24 (the number of months we would be living in Poland) to get $833. Every month, before we had a chance to spend this $833, we had it automatically deducted from our checking account into our savings. After two years, we returned home with $20,000!

Our salaries were comparable to what we earned in the States and, since the cost of living was low in Poland (at least compared to America's standards), we were able to travel and still save money. We were fortunate to have these opportunities, but we also took some risks. We moved to a country that was far away from home. We didn't know the language and encountered some pretty sticky situations. But sometimes we all have to step out of our comfort zones to achieve growth.

After moving back home, we were able to apply a 20% down payment on our first house and furnish it without using credit. At this point, we sat down and discussed our financial goals again. We felt strongly about having Tracy be able to stay home for at least one year when we had a child. These matters are ultimately up to the Man Upstairs, but we planned on having Tracy work one year and then get pregnant. In order to make it on my teacher's salary as our sole source of income, we would have to be pretty much debt-free.

We were planning on buying two cars like most couples do, but this would derail our plans of being out of debt by the time we had a baby. We decided to go with one car with the hopes of paying it off in full in two years. I landed a job close to home and Tracy taught at another school not too far away either. Most mornings I would drop her off at work and then go to mine. There were days that she needed the car after school and I would have to ride my bike to school. A lot of people thought this was weird. They actually made fun of me. This is a big reason many folks go into debt—they try too hard to impress others.

Now, I certainly didn't enjoy the ridicule, but since I had my eyes on a bigger goal, I just let the insults rub off. As a side note, some of these same people who made fun of me found themselves in financial trouble a few years later. I didn't feel good about this but it definitely shows that if broke people are laughing at you then you must be doing something right.

Since we only had one car payment, Tracy and I paid extra on this each month. I am happy to say it was paid off in full two years later. At this point in time we also had Tracy's student loan debt. We paid extra on this debt too and, by the time Ava was born, we were debt-free and able to have Tracy stay home with her.

⎯ *Add More to Your Emergency Fund* ⎯

You now have no debt except your mortgage or rent and have around $2,000 in an emergency fund. Next, add enough money to this fund to cover three to six months' worth of living expenses—enough money to live your life if you went without income for this amount of time. Remember, this money is meant to be used for emergencies and not to earn a lot of interest. You also want this money to be sufficiently accessible.

Should you save three or six months' worth of living expenses? That's a personal decision. Since I am currently the only breadwinner in my house and have three other people who need food, clothing and shelter relying on me, I went for six months. My family relies solely on my income and—let's face it—we never know when that pink slip could come.

I feel pretty secure in my job but there have been teachers at my school who have been laid off. It was devastating for them, and I would find it devastating if it happened to me. Yet it would be much worse if I didn't have any money set aside for a situation just like this. Having this cushion enables me to sleep peacefully at night knowing I would have time to look for another job and still feed my family if the unthinkable happened.

⸻ *Invest* ⸻

The next step is to start investing in retirement accounts. Now, I know that some folks don't trust the stock market and would rather put their money under their mattresses. Let me explain why investing in stocks and mutual funds is a great way to build wealth.

It's well known that a lot of people lost huge sums of money in the recent stock market crash. If you turned on any of the national news shows in late 2008 and early 2009, you would have thought the sky was falling. There were reports of people losing everything, but for most people this wasn't true. On October 9, 2007, the Dow Jones Industrial Average closed at a high of 14,164. Fast-forward to March 9, 2009: the Dow closed at 6,547. A huge loss for sure but people didn't lose all their money. Some lost over half but not all.

While many were saying to get out of stocks and mutual funds at this time, I was actually okay with them dropping in value. In my opinion, money invested in stocks and mutual funds should stay invested for the long haul—at least 10 years. I am no financial genius and cannot predict how the market will perform in the future but I look at the past and feel confident.

From January 1871 through December 2009, the Dow Jones Industrial Average averaged 10.5% growth each year. This time frame encompassed two World Wars, the Great Depression and the tragedy of 9/11. Based on this past performance, I'm pretty sure that the money I invest will continue to grow.

Let's say you see a sweater at Macy's that costs $50. This is too much for you so you choose not to buy it. Two weeks later it goes on sale for half-off. At this price, you might consider buying it. That is the way I view the stock market. When it's down, I look at it like I'm buying stocks and mutual funds on sale.

Here's something I bet you didn't hear in the media during the recent downturn. Let's say you invested $1,000,000 in the stock market on that dreadful March day in 2009. Did you know that by December of 2010 that $1,000,000 would be worth almost $2,000,000? Your favorite morning show probably didn't mention that. We all know that bad news sells so this is probably the reason that many shows did not point this out. For example, now that gasoline is approaching $4 per gallon again (as I write this), the media is constantly reminding us of this. When gas was selling below $2 per gallon no one discussed it. Just remember that many media outlets like to dramatize events; do not let this scare you into doing nothing to prepare for your future.

The *Washington Post*, Harvard University and the Kaiser Family Foundation recently conducted a study on race and investing. They divided their subjects into three ethnic groups (whites, blacks and Hispanics) to determine the percentage of each who owned any stocks, bonds or mutual funds. It came out as follows:

Whites	49%
Blacks	25%
Hispanics	16%

Pretty alarming, huh? In these days of lost pensions and government cutbacks, a majority of Americans are still depending on Uncle Sam to support them in their golden years. We've got to start taking control of our lives and money so that we're not dependent on others to support us when we can no longer work.

To begin investing, seek out someone you feel handles his/her money well. Take them out for coffee and ask how they invest their money and who they use to make these investments. You can then meet with a financial advisor and interview him/her to make sure he/she has your best interests at heart. Once you find the correct person for you, the investing can start.

Tracy and I met with a financial advisor whom our local school district recommended at our teacher orientation meeting. Some school districts hire an investment consulting and financial firm to select the best company to represent the district and its employees when it comes to retirement planning. These firms have no bias towards a particular company/advisor and gather information from numerous companies to make the best choice for the district. Even if this is the case for you, I highly recommend you do some research before automatically just going with the company/advisor your district selected.

After this meeting, we scheduled an appointment to see if we felt comfortable with this advisor managing our money. We did and started investing a relatively little amount—$100—each month. We have increased this monthly amount as we got raises. We used (and still use) a strategy known as dollar-cost averaging. Each month we have a set amount automatically deducted into our retirement accounts. This money is taken out before we have a chance to see it and, thus, spend it.

Too many of us spend our entire paychecks (if not more). This is why it's so important to have this money taken out before you have a chance to get used to it as income. Using this approach, you're not trying to time the market. You are investing for the long haul and will use the magic of compound interest to build wealth.

Let's say you use this approach beginning at age 25. You invest $200 each month and earn 10% a year on this investment. How much do you think you'll have by the time you're 65? Drum roll, please: over $1,118,000! Not too bad.

There are many types of vehicles you can use including Roth IRAs, 401(k)s and 403(b)s. A professional can help you select the best option. But remember, the person who cares the most about your money and your future is the one who looks back at you each morning in the mirror.

Save for College

Wow, now you have no debt, a three-to-six-month emergency fund in place and are investing for the future. Now it's time to think about the kiddos. College planning can be confusing given all of the options available. You can save for college by investing in ESAs (Educational Savings Accounts), 529s and even Roth IRAs. I highly recommend you talk this over with your financial advisor so you can choose the best option for your child(ren).

Tracy and I started this after Ava was born; we now invest for Ella too. We are not able to invest a lot but feel that something is better than nothing. We're making an investment in them right now by having Tracy stay home but hope we'll be able to cover some of their college expenses too. We use a Roth IRA for this investment.

With a Roth, you can take out the money invested (not the interest earned on this money) with no penalty. You have to use an ESA for schooling or take a penalty. What if Ava and Ella both get full scholarships? By having their college money in a Roth IRA, Tracy and I would be able to use this to help them pay for their wedding or a down payment on their first house *or* use it for our retirements without paying a penalty. Once again, refer to a professional to help you make the correct decision for you and your family.

When planning for college, think about the value you're getting for your money. As a schoolteacher, I would make the same amount whether I have a degree from Yale or from the University of Georgia. According to the College Board, the average price for tuition and fees in 2010 is as follows:

Private 4-year college	$27,293
Public 4-year college (in-state)	$7,605
Public 2-year college	$2,713

I myself attended a community college for two years then graduated with my bachelor's degree from a state university and no one has ever held this against me. There are degrees from some universities that mean more than others but, in many careers, a degree is a degree no matter where one attended.

One final note. Notice that investing for your children comes *after* investing for yourself. I know as parents we usually put our children's needs first and want to give them everything we can. Here is one area where you need to be selfish and put yourself before your kids.

Imagine this scenario: let's say you didn't follow these steps in the order I've described. You are able to pay for their college in full and they graduate and get great jobs. They then marry and begin having children of their own. You are now getting older and ready to retire but cannot because you haven't saved enough. One day the boss comes in and tells you thanks for your service but the company no longer needs you. What will you do now?

Unfortunately, many parents get into this situation and have to move in with their children. I am sure Ava and Ella love me dearly but I don't want to put them in such a situation. It is my goal to be able to pay for their college but I am not sacrificing my retirement to do so. They could do well in high school and earn a scholarship. They might have to work during college and not live in the fanciest dorm. If worse comes to worst, they may have to get a student loan. I don't want them to have to get a loan but at least they have that option; the last time I checked, there is no option for a retirement loan.

There is a recently released book by Zac Bissonnette entitled *Debt-Free U: How I Paid for an Outstanding College Education Without Loans, Scholarships, or Mooching off My Parents* that might be interesting for you to read. This book offers firsthand advice on how to pay for college without taking out loans. The author feels that students should pay for most of their education expenses by working while in college and during breaks. He also feels that attending community college for two years before transferring to a four-year college or university would go a long way towards cutting costs (something that worked well for me). He also offers convincing research showing that elite graduate programs and selective employers accept plenty of people who have attended non-elite schools. This might be a valuable resource for those of you looking to cut college costs.

⁓ *Lose the Mortgage* ⁓

This is where the fun really begins. Look around your home, in your garage, out your backdoor. Imagine the feeling of owning it all, free and clear. Now is the time to get rid of that last debt—your mortgage.

Many people assume they will always have a house payment and don't realize how much interest they're paying on their loans. Let's say you buy a house for $150,000. You make a down payment of $30,000 so you take out a 30-year mortgage for $120,000 with a 5% interest rate. Your monthly payment would be $644. To find out the true cost of this $150,000 house we'll do some math. Paying $644/month adds up to $7,728 each year ($644 x 12). Take that $7,728 and multiply it by 30 years to get $231,840. Add your $30,000 down payment to this amount and your $150,000 house will cost you $261,840 when all is said and done!

There are a few ways you can pay off your mortgage faster. You can promise yourself that you will pay extra each month towards this loan and sign up for a 30-year loan. If you're serious about paying your home off early, this is probably not the best option. Most of us make promises that we cannot keep. We might have the best intentions to pay extra each month but then something comes up—Valentine's Day in February, summer vacation in July, Christmas in December—and we find we need this "extra" money.

If you do have a 30-year loan, you could sign up to make biweekly payments instead of a monthly payment. These biweekly payments will be half of what your monthly payment is but you'll actually be making an "extra" payment each year. Here is how this works. Let's say your monthly payment is $1,000. You will pay $12,000 each year towards your mortgage: 12 (months in a year) times $1,000 (monthly payment) = $12,000. If you used the biweekly approach, you'll pay $500 (half of the monthly $1,000 payment) every two weeks. There are 52 weeks in a year so you'll make 26 half payments. $500 times 26 equals $13,000; thus, you will make one extra $1,000 payment each year.

Doing this can trim anywhere from five to seven years off your 30-year loan depending on the terms. One warning about this approach—be careful that your mortgage company doesn't charge a fee for this. Some of them try to slip this in so just make sure yours does not do this to you.

The easiest way to pay off your loan might be to refinance. As I write this, interest rates are very low. My family moved from Florida to Georgia in the summer of 2006. We ended up going with a 30-year loan. Two years later, interest rates dropped and we refinanced. We were able to lower our rate by a full two points and reduced our term from 30 years to 15 years. We pay around $150 more each month compared to our original loan but will own our house free and clear much earlier and save almost $100,000. Not everyone is eligible to refinance but it's something definitely worth looking into.

I have heard some arguments against paying off your mortgage early. One is that you won't be able to take the home mortgage interest deduction and reduce your taxable income. First off, in order to claim this credit, you must itemize your deductions which a majority of Americans do not do; most take the standard deduction.

Let's say you do itemize and can claim this deduction. We'll say you're in the 25% income tax bracket. You have a 30-year, $200,000 mortgage with a 5% interest rate. You would pay your mortgage company $10,000 a year in interest (5% of $200,000 is $10,000). Now for your big write-off. Since you're in the 25% tax bracket, you'll be able to write off 25% of the interest you paid on your mortgage.

Using the above-mentioned numbers, your write-off would be $2,500 (25% of $10,000 equals $2,500). So, if you think you should keep your mortgage because of this deduction, you are basically saying that one should pay $10,000 a year in interest to his/her mortgage company so this person can reduce his/her taxable income by $2,500. I am no mathematical genius, but paying $10,000 to save $2,500 doesn't make much sense to me. If you find someone who likes this math, please give him/her my contact information and I will gladly write them a check for $2,500 in exchange for $10,000.

Another argument I've heard against paying off a mortgage early is that one could invest this money and earn more in the stock market. That is hard to argue against because it is true. If your mortgage rate is 5% and you pay it off early you will, in essence, be earning 5% a year. As mentioned before, the stock market averages over 10% growth a year so, mathematically, paying extra towards your principal instead of investing this amount is not wise.

Here is where we have to take a look at the bigger picture. Since this is the case, why don't more people take out a home equity loan and invest all of this in mutual funds? One could borrow money at a 5% set interest rate and earn over 10% on this same money by investing it—sounds like a no-brainer to me. Once again, here is where we need to take a look at the emotional impact of such a decision.

Most people will not do this because they don't view their house as just an investment—it is a huge part of who they are. In fact, according to a 2011 poll conducted by Allstate/The National Journal Heartland Monitor, the best reasons for home ownership are:

Having a place to raise a family	40%
Building equity rather than paying rent	26%
Making a good long-term investment	13%
Acquiring an asset you can pass along	9%
Being part of a neighborhood and community	6%
Following in your parents' footsteps	2%
Getting a tax deduction	2%

While you could invest this money, imagine the feeling of owning all of your possessions! I bet the grass in your backyard feels a lot different when you own it.

⸺ *Do Whatever You Want* ⸺

You are now in the position to pretty much do anything you want. Let's say you go to work one Monday morning and your boss is in your ear and you have had enough. Since you don't have many bills, you are now in the position that you can look for a more fulfilling job— even if it doesn't pay as much as your current one. You can also save up fast and buy that sports car you've always wanted to drive. The options for having fun are almost unlimited.

You can also continue to have your money grow. If you've wanted to become a landlord, now is the time. Since you have no mortgage, you'll be able to handle paying a mortgage on your rental house if it is unoccupied for a period of time.

Once you're in this position, the greatest thing you'll be able to do is give away some of your money. I am not a big fan of others telling me I have to give them some of my hard-earned money, but it feels a little different when you're able to willingly give.

Think of two of the wealthiest people on Earth: Bill Gates and Oprah Winfrey. These two have made more money than you and I ever will. They can pretty much buy (and probably have bought) anything they want. However, when they talk about what gives them the greatest joy, it has nothing to do with things they bought for themselves.

Bill Gates is most proud of his foundation that has helped countless individuals across the world. One of Oprah's greatest accomplishments is the school she created in South Africa. Things come and go, but helping others can create a legacy that lasts generations. In my own life, I am forever grateful to my Great-great-uncle Jimmy and my grandmother.

Uncle Jimmy left my grandmother a small sum of money when he passed away a number of years ago.

Instead of blowing this money and using it all on herself, my grandmother used it to help pay for some of my college expenses. She also used some of it to help my brother attend fire school and become a firefighter. Thanks to these unselfish acts, I was able to become a teacher and have an impact on hundreds of students, and Kyle was able to become a fireman and paramedic and save countless lives. I hope that Uncle Jimmy is smiling down at us knowing that he is still making this world a better place.

CHAPTER 6
Continue Educating Yourself about Finances

My goal in writing this book is to help you manage your money better and gain control over your life. I hope at this point you're excited about what you've learned, and would like to keep learning more about finances and money. Here are some resources I highly recommend to help you further your understanding.

Books

As you've been reading this book, do these steps seem familiar to you? They're aligned with the teachings of Dave Ramsey. I mentioned him on page 53. Dave is host of his own radio program, *The Dave Ramsey Show*, that is heard on over 180 radio stations throughout the United States and is also the author of numerous financial books.

I had never even heard of him until a few years ago. After listening to his show, I realized we were pretty much taking the same steps he recommends. And the proof is in the pudding—the steps I've described in this book have worked for us and countless others.

The Traveler's Gift	Andy Andrews
The Automatic Millionaire	David Bach
The Wealthy Barber	David Chilton
The Richest Man in Babylon	George Clason
Your Money or Your Life	Joe Dominguez and Vicki Robin
The Science of Getting Rich	Nathan Hill
Get Clark Smart: The Ultimate Guide for the Savvy Consumer	Clark Howard
Who Moved My Cheese	Spencer Johnson
Smart Is the New Rich	Christine Romans
The Total Money Makeover	Dave Ramsey
The Millionaire Next Door	Dr. Thomas Stanley

Financial Books for Children

The Ant and the Grasshopper	Aesop
The Berenstain Bears Think of Those in Need	Stan and Jan Berenstain
The Super Red Racer	Dave Ramsey
Careless at the Carnival	Dave Ramsey
The Big Birthday Surprise	Dave Ramsey
My Fantastic Fieldtrip	Dave Ramsey
A Special Thank You	Dave Ramsey
Battle of the Chores	Dave Ramsey
If You Made a Million Dollars	David Schwartz
The Giving Tree	Shel Silverstein
Alexander Who Used to Be Rich Last Sunday	Judith Viorst

Websites

www.bankrate.com
www.getrichslowly.com
www.onemoneydesign.com
www.thesimpledollar.com

Radio Shows

The Clark Howard Show
Crown Financial's MoneyLife
The Dave Ramsey Show

Television Shows

The Clark Howard Show on HLN
The Suze Orman Show on CNBC
Your Bottom Line on CNN
Your $$$$ on CNN
The Fox Business Network (various shows)

CHAPTER 7
Giving Your Children a Financial Education

I feel that children can start learning about money early. Once my older daughter, Ava, turned three we had her doing simple household chores so we could teach her how to handle money.

I first must begin by saying that I am not a fan of rewarding others for things they should be doing. I did, however, make an exception with Ava since my initial goal was to teach her money management skills. We started with chores that were easy for her to complete: cleaning her room, brushing her teeth, and so on. Every night we would check off the chores that were completed, and every Friday we added them up and she was paid. We called this money what most parents do: an allowance. There are other parents who feel it should be called a commission or such since one has to produce to get paid. No matter what you call it, make sure your child does the work to earn the money.

After Ava got paid (she could earn up to $1 each week), she had three jars: one labeled *Give Away*, one *Savings* and the other *Spending*. She first put 10 cents in the *Give Away* jar, 25 cents in the *Savings* jar and the remaining amount in the *Spending* jar. This worked so well for us. When we were at the store, often Ava would see something she wanted. We never had any arguments; we would simply say, "We'll have to go home and see if you have enough money in your spending and/or savings jar to buy it."

Ava has used the money in her *Give Away* jar in numerous ways. One year there was a little girl at my school who lost her father shortly before Christmas. Ava used her *Give Away* money to buy this little girl a stuffed animal. Ava actually came to my school and delivered this to her personally. Another year, Ava used this money to buy canned food for needy families in our community. This past Christmas, there was a family at her school that was struggling. Ava used the money in her *Give Away* jar to buy them a gift card to a local grocery store.

Ava uses the money in her *Savings* jar to buy things that cost a few weeks' worth of allowance. We let her use her *Spending* jar for anything she wants. Sometimes I have to bite my tongue because some of the things she buys are junk. I refrain from saying anything because I would rather her make mistakes now and only blow a couple of bucks than wait until she is older when those same mistakes may be much more costly.

Recently, Ava showed that these lessons in money management are paying off. Twice a year the media center at her school hosts a book fair. The children get very excited and want to buy almost everything they see—it's almost like Black Friday for kids. Last year, Ava came home after visiting the book fair and had to have a Taylor Swift book.

Now, with her mom and dad both being former first-grade teachers, she probably has 2,000 books. It was hard for me not to say anything but we looked in her *Savings* jar and she had enough for this book—$5. The next day she brought her money to school to purchase it.

When she got home that afternoon, she still had the $5 in her backpack. We asked why she didn't buy the book and Ava told us that it had sold out and was no longer for sale. I was shocked—most kids (and adults too) would have that money burn a hole in their pocket and would've moved on and bought something else.

Here's where the story gets *really* good. The next day, the media specialist called and said they had found some more copies of this book. She told me she would set one aside for Ava. Later that day, I told Ava the good news. She was thrilled.

It was a wonderful learning opportunity for Ava. I told her many people would have spent their money on something they didn't really want and, when the item they originally were going to buy became available, they wouldn't be able to purchase it. They might even do something foolish and buy this item on credit. This situation showed me that some of what I was teaching Ava was, in fact, sinking in.

When Ava turned six, I changed the way she was paid and how she was able to earn her allowance. I explained to her that the chores she once got paid for doing were now actions she was expected to do as a member of our family. The upside was she could now get a raise and earn $1.50 each week.

To earn this money, she would have to gather the garbage around the house every Sunday and clean her bathroom—this included cleaning her mirror and sink and scrubbing the toilet—once a week. Now that she had a basic understanding of money management, I wanted to teach her that going above and beyond can pay off. (I am fairly certain that not many six-year-olds scrub their toilets.)

I feel if Ava continues to apply these lessons in life—gives away 10% of her money, then saves 25% of it and uses the remainder for spending—and goes above and beyond in her job, she will be wealthy in more ways than a fat bank account can show.

Tips for Teens

Teach Self-Control

It is so important that we learn how to delay gratification. Many of us do not set long-term goals and instead spend money on things that we truly don't need. Help your teen develop a plan that will give measurable results. For example, have him/her make a goal of saving $25 each month. This is something that is achievable for most but also easy to keep track of.

Help Them Take Control of Their Futures

If you don't learn how to manage your own money, others will find ways to do it for you. (Bernie Madoff, anyone?) This is a great time to start talking to your child about money. Sit down with them and go over your bills together. Show them why they cannot have everything their friends have and that you're not saying no because you are just so mean. Let them see how much the mortgage and electric bills are. Many families never discuss financial matters—some are even more comfortable talking about the birds and bees than finances. Don't miss this valuable opportunity to teach your child(ren) about money.

The Value of Work

Having a car is a major expense for most teens. My parents taught me a great lesson when I was looking to buy my first car. I began working when I was 14 years old. My family owned an appliance business and I delivered and set up appliances during my summer break. My parents agreed to match the amount I earned and I could apply this towards my car. Instead of hanging out with my friends all summer, I lifted heavy appliances in the hot Florida sun. I continued to do this in the afternoons once school started.

By the time I turned 16, I had saved $2,000! With my parents matching this amount, I had enough to buy a $4,000 car. My grandfather was looking to purchase a new vehicle and was kind enough to sell me his truck for the amount I had. This was my first real understanding of money. I realized that if I worked hard and saved, I could buy something that I desired.

I was fortunate that my parents gave me money but even more fortunate that they made me work to earn this amount. Some of my friends had their cars and other items bought for them by their parents and, let me tell you, they did not treat their possessions like I did mine. I valued what I had because I knew how much sweat had gone into earning it.

Balancing a Checkbook

This is a great time to start teaching your children about balancing a checkbook. Jump$tart Coalition did a survey on financial literacy with high school students. According to this study, only 45% of the high school seniors surveyed had a checking account. Once they go off to college and are more or less on their own, they begin making mistakes. 30% of college students surveyed admitted to bouncing a check.

Once your child gets a job and/or begins earning money, take them to a bank to open checking and savings accounts. Teach them how to write a check and balance a checkbook. They can even get a debit card to help them manage their money better. Don't wait until they are on their own, when financial mistakes can be more costly.

Discuss Wants Versus Needs

Many teens (as well as adults) think that certain things are absolute needs when, in fact, they are not. The teenage years are a good time to discuss this since many teens feel they just *have* to have something because someone else does. 11% of high school students surveyed by the Jump-$tart Coalition thought it was okay to borrow money to buy clothing or go on vacation. I suggest you discuss this with your teen sooner rather than later.

In fact, you can begin this discussion when your child is quite young. When Ava was five, she really wanted a Nintendo DS for Christmas. Tracy and I didn't have this in our Christmas budget. Even though I'm pretty frugal I have to admit I thought hard about buying this for her. After all, Christmas only comes once a year and she was a good girl and she didn't want a lot of other things and she was doing well in school and ... I could go on and on with reasons she should have a DS and justify buying it for her. Tracy and I finally sat down to really discuss it and came to the conclusion that since it exceeded the amount we had set aside, the DS would have to wait for later.

Christmas came and went and Ava enjoyed all of the gifts she received. She did mention that maybe she could get a DS for her birthday but that was it. She was not devastated and will not need counseling because she did not receive this present. The very Sunday after Christmas, our heat went out and we had to have someone come and repair our unit. The interesting thing is that the bill was a little over the amount we would have spent on a DS. How weird is that? I then used this as a teaching opportunity, explaining to Ava why we have an emergency fund set up and how we don't use this money for wants—like a Nintendo DS.

Learn about Uncle Sam

Many adults, let alone teens, know almost nothing about taxes. Once your child earns his/her first paycheck, sit down with him/her and explain to them what's on their pay stub. Talk to them about federal, state, Social Security and Medicare taxes. When it comes time to file a tax return, have them sit down with you (or your accountant) so they can learn about this too.

Save for the Future

Many teens lack the ability to see one week into the future so getting them to think about retirement can be difficult. However, now is a great time to teach them about compound interest. Here is a comparison which shows why it's important to start investing early:

John and Jeremy were friends since they were little. As they got older, they both knew they should start thinking about their futures. When John turned 19, he decided to invest $2,000 every year (under $167 a month) for eight years. He picked mutual funds that averaged a 12% interest rate. Once he hit 26, John stopped investing. So he put a total of $16,000 into his investment funds.

Jeremy waited until he had a better-paying job at age 27 before saving for retirement. Just like John, he put $2,000 into his investment funds every year until he turned 65. He earned the same 12% interest rate as John but invested 31 more years than John did. He ended up investing a total of $78,000 over 39 years.

Fast forward to when they both turned 65. Who do you think had more? John, with his total of $16,000 invested over eight years, or Jeremy, who invested $78,000 over 39 years? It turns out John came out way ahead! Jeremy had a total of $1,532,166, while John had a total of $2,288,996. How is this possible? Well, John had the power of compound interest on his side longer than Jeremy and, thus, came out over $700,000 ahead of Jeremy even though he invested a lot less.

Here's an easy way to teach your kids about compound interest. Let's say you invest $100 and this investment averages a 9% return a year. Because of compound interest this money will double in eight years. The chart below shows you how this works.

Year	Money Earned from Interest	Total Amount of Money
0	$0.00	$100.00
1	$9.00 (9% of $100.00)	$109.00
2	$9.81 (9% of $109.00)	$118.81
3	$10.69 (9% of $118.81)	$129.50
4	$11.66 (9% of $129.50)	$141.16
5	$12.70 (9% of $141.16)	$153.86
6	$13.85 (9% of $153.86)	$167.71
7	$15.09 (9% of $167.71)	$182.80
8	$16.45 (9% of $182.80)	$199.26

Now they can see how a small amount of money can turn into a lot.

— *Tips for Young Adults* —

Find Your Purpose

Most of us were born with certain talents and abilities. Discuss potential career choices with your child to help him/her choose a path that best suits him/her. I feel like I was given a gift to teach, both in school and in giving financial advice to others. Even though teaching doesn't pay a large salary, I am very content.

Talk with your child about finding purpose in life. Encourage him/her to pursue a career that is rewarding and not just one that pays a large salary.

Place a Value on Money

Money doesn't always buy happiness but it can definitely eliminate things that would make you unhappy. Teach your child that money is what you earn in exchange for your time doing a particular job.

Let's say your child earns $10 an hour at his/her job. He/she wants to buy an iPad that costs $500. Explain that, in order to buy this iPad, he/she will have to work over 50 hours to buy it. When you look at it this way, it makes you think a little differently before spending your hard-earned money.

Choose Your Partner Wisely

While you are dating it's very easy to fall in love and not recognize the differences between you and your partner. Get to really know your soul mate and find out about his/her ethical and moral values. This is also the time to discuss how you each view finances. Opposites do attract and in a typical relationship, one partner is usually the saver and the other a spender. That is okay as long as you see eye-to-eye on the major financial issues.

In our marriage, Tracy was more of the spender and I was the saver. Over time, we've helped each other see things from the other person's point-of-view. Tracy is actually tighter with money than I am now and I have become a little less frugal.

A few years ago, Tracy made a skeleton costume for Ava. She used white felt for the bones and glued these onto an inexpensive $5 t-shirt. Shortly after Ava came home from trick-or-treating, I walked into our living room and saw Tracy trying to peel these bones off the t-shirt. I asked why she was doing this and she said it was a perfectly fine t- shirt and was trying to save it. I laughed and said, "We can afford to buy a new shirt." Tracy replied, "Why buy another shirt and spend money when I can make this one as good as new?"

Be Prepared for the Unexpected

When talking with young people about money, be sure to discuss the importance of having an emergency fund. They need to realize that the unexpected does happen. They may lose a job or need a major repair done on their car. Explain that an emergency fund is completely different from a retirement fund. They should try to never use their retirement accounts to pay for emergencies.

Let's say that Jim decides to invest instead of setting up an emergency fund. One day he needs a new air conditioning unit that costs $10,000. He uses his 401(k) to pay for this. If Jim is in the 25% income tax bracket, using $10,000 from this account will cost him $2,500 in taxes plus another $1,000 in a penalty for using this money too early. This $10,000 is now worth $6,500 because Jim did not prepare. Help your child avoid making this kind of mistake.

Finance College

Many young adults don't think twice about racking up large student debts. I know that for some people, getting a student loan is the only way they'll be able to attend college, so it can be a good investment for many, but I would advise you to sit down with your teen and explain how these loans work.

Many college students do not work, so they take out enough to pay for their living expenses as well as tuition and other student fees. I encourage you to explain to them that they'll have to start paying towards this loan once they graduate, when they're just starting out in life and will have many other expenses to worry about.

If your child does need to obtain a student loan, my advice is that they use it for educational expenses only and get a job to pay for their living expenses.

Ava recently showed me that you might even be able to discuss this with your child(ren) way before they start applying for college—she recently finished first grade. During the last week of school, her school had Award's Day for the students. Ava got a gold medal (it was real gold according to her) for exceeding in all academic areas. Not many of her peers obtained this so I was very proud of her for working so hard at school.

The next morning, on our way to school, I told

Ava how proud I was of her and started to discuss the importance of getting good grades and giving her best effort. I know college is far off but it will be here before we know it. I told Ava that if she continues to do well until she graduates from high school, she will have more options on where she can go to college. I also told her that a college might even pay for her to attend their school. Ava then said, "That's called a scholarship." My mouth about dropped to the floor—we were on to something here. I then went further and explained that if she did not get a scholarship she could still go to college but would probably have to work or get a student loan. Tracy and I do invest for both our daughters' college, but may not have enough to cover the entire tuition ourselves.

I went on to tell her that once she graduates and gets a job, she will have to start paying this loan off. Ava then said, "I will actually have to pay more than the amount the loan was for." Now I was really in shock. I asked her how she knew this and she replied, "Most people don't just give you money for free—you have to pay them more since they let you borrow it." At this point I did not know what to say. My seven-year-old knows more about student loans than many college freshmen do.

When I got to school, I called Tracy to let her know about our conversation. It turns out, Ava and Tracy had a similar conversation the day before. We discuss money topics with our children as often as we can. We talk openly about how much I make and the bills that we have. I know some of the things we talk about are over our daughters' heads, but this conversation showed me that maybe they actually understand more than what I think they do. As a teacher, I know we don't teach enough financial skills to our students. If you are a parent it is so important to discuss money with your child(ren) when the opportunity presents itself—you never know the impact it will have.

Discuss Debt

Many young adults accumulate debt buying pizza or their beverage of choice without thinking about the future ramifications of this debt. Even though paying the minimum looks very affordable, you have to plug in the numbers to discover the true cost of debt. If someone charges $3,000 on a credit card with an 18% interest rate and just pays the minimum amount each month, it will take almost 22 years to get rid of this debt!

In fact, according to the report "How Undergraduate Students Use Credit Cards: Sallie Mae's National Study of Usage Rates and Trends, 2009," nearly one-third (30%) of college students put tuition on their credit card in 2008. In addition, 92% of undergraduate credit cardholders charged textbooks, school supplies or other direct education expenses. Students who used credit cards to pay for direct education expenses estimated charging $2,200.

84% of undergraduates had at least one credit card. On average, students have 4.6 credit cards, and half of college students had four or more cards. The average balance of this debt was $3,173.

The higher the grade level, the more heavily students used their credit cards, with seniors graduating with an average credit card debt of more than $4,100. The study found that freshmen carried a median debt of $939 and only 15% of freshmen had a zero credit card balance.

Many college students seem to use credit cards to live beyond their means—not just for convenience—and more than three-quarters incurred finance charges by carrying a monthly balance.

This study also found that:

- 60% experienced surprise at how high their balance had reached and 40% said they've charged items knowing they did not have the money to pay the bill.

- Only 17% said they regularly paid off all cards each month, and another 1% had parents, a spouse, or other family members paying the bill. The remaining 82% carried balances and thus incurred finance charges each month.

- Two-thirds of survey respondents said they had frequently or sometimes discussed credit card use with their parents. The remaining one-third who had never or only rarely discussed credit cards with parents were more likely to pay for tuition with a credit card and were more likely to be surprised at their credit card balance when they received the invoice.

- 84% percent of undergraduates indicated they needed more education on financial management topics. In fact, 64% would have liked to receive information in high school and 40% as college freshmen.

Don't let your child be in the majority—explain how debt works so they don't ending up feeling like the 84% who need more financial management education.

DANNY KOFKE

CHAPTER 8
Living Well with Little Money: Live the Life You Want *(Even on a Moderate Income)*

Close your eyes and think back to when you were six years old. What did you want to be when you got older? What did your future look like at this point in time? When I was six, I was going to be the next Dale Murphy, roaming center field for the Atlanta Braves. Life is so magical at that age because we dream big and think we can be anything we want to. Most of us had few limitations and weren't faced with the difficult, or even devastating, life challenges we sometimes encounter as adults.

I was recently reminded of this by six-year-old Ava. A few months ago she came home from school very excited. She told Tracy and me that she learned to use PowerPoint at school. She then got on our laptop and, 20 minutes later, had indeed created a short presentation.

I didn't learn how to create a PowerPoint presentation until I was in my thirties and fought it tooth and nail. Yet here was my six-year-old, excited to learn and try something new. It was so cool to see how open-minded Ava was and how much fun she had. I know that as we age we are less open to change because we have so much on our plates. If you're serious about changing your financial situation and, thus, your life, you might have to tap into that six-year-old mind-set that is buried deep down in most of us.

As we get older, a lot of us want more but settle for less. We stop dreaming and tell ourselves we'll be happy once certain things happen. We fool ourselves and think, "Once I make $10,000 more a year I'll be content" or "When I get rid of this beater and drive a new car my life will be better." When these things finally happen, we *are* happy—for a moment. However, this feeling of happiness eventually fades and we're right back where we started. True happiness doesn't come from things, it comes from action and doing things that bring long-lasting satisfaction, not just a temporary fix.

After reading this book, I hope you are ready to make that change (if you need to) and start living life to the fullest. Maybe you're thinking, "I wish I could do it, but the cards are stacked against me." Or you perceive other roadblocks in your way, keeping you from changing: "I'm too old to change" or "There's no way I can do these steps" or "I have a family to support by myself." It's easy to come up with excuses. The secret is to look for the reasons and ways we *can* achieve our goals.

The Finish Line

I have run numerous 5K races and hope to one day run a half-marathon and maybe even a full marathon. While training for these races, the hardest step I take is always the first one. There are some days I think there is no way I'll even be able to run 100 feet let alone three miles.

But after I take that first step, I realize I don't feel as bad as I originally thought and the next thing I know, my run is almost over. The same might be true for you on this financial journey. No matter how difficult it might be, you owe it to yourself to not give up and to finish this race.

There might be some falls and some days that you just feel like throwing in the towel but don't—you can do this!

I once read that the best time to plant an oak tree was 20 years ago and the next best time is today. I hope that you are now motivated to go out, get that shovel and start planting. Good luck and God bless!

⟋ *Financial Success Against All Odds* ⟍

It can be really inspiring to learn about people who have achieved their goals despite facing long odds. Here are some of my favorites.

Colonel Sanders
Never Too Old to Fry a Chicken

When Harland Sanders was five, his father died and with his mother at work all day, Harland took over the cooking and cleaning for his family. He dropped out of school in seventh grade and, after his mother remarried, he ran away from home. At 16 he falsified his birth date and enlisted in the army. After his service commitment was up, he held various jobs including insurance salesman, steamboat pilot farmer and railroad fireman. He never had much success with these jobs and failure seemed to follow him wherever he went.

He got married, but that too was not a success. After a bitter argument, his wife took their two daughters to her mother's house. Harland was very upset and decided he was going to kidnap his daughters. He planned to hide in the bushes outside his mother-in-law's house and when his daughters came outside he would take them. He waited a long time, but they didn't come outside. He had failed again.

At the age of 40, Harland began cooking chicken dishes for people who stopped at his service station in Kentucky. His popularity increased and he moved to a restaurant where he worked as the chef. As this restaurant started to become successful, a newly paved interstate was completed. This interstate bypassed Harland's restaurant and it eventually failed. Harland was 65 years old. He had just received his first Social Security check.

A lot of people might have given up at this point, but Harland didn't. He took the $105 check and began talking with potential franchisees. He found one that liked his idea. This restaurant took off and Harland became known as Colonel Sanders. In 1964, Sanders sold the Kentucky Fried Chicken Corporation for $2 million.

Here was a man who didn't let previous failures or his age hold him back from his dream.

Mike Tomlin
Coaching in the Steel City

Mike Tomlin graduated from William and Mary College in 1995. He had played wide receiver but, after graduating, had little hopes of playing in the NFL. He had three choices in front of him. He was studying for the LSAT, with the possibility of going to law school. He had an offer to sell insurance with an annual starting salary of around $65,000. His third choice was to take a graduate-assistant coaching job at Virginia Military Institute, live in a dorm and make $12,000 a year.

This decision seemed pretty easy, right? He should either go to law school or sell insurance. To the dismay of his parents—they did send him to one of the best colleges in the country—Mike decided to take the low-paying graduate-assistant job. Many of his friends were going on to law school or well-paying jobs but Tomlin wanted to follow his dreams.

He loved football and wanted to find a way to make a living coaching. He believed that success is not measured in money but rather in the mark you leave in the world.

After his stint at VMI, he coached at the University of Memphis, Tennessee-Martin, Arkansas State University and the University of Cincinnati. He then moved on to the NFL and coached under Tony Dungy and Jon Gruden with the Tampa Bay Buccaneers and then for one year as the defensive coordinator with the Minnesota Vikings.

At the conclusion of the 2006–07 football season, Bill Cowher stepped down as head coach for the Pittsburgh Steelers. Tomlin decided to interview for this position. The Steelers had just won the Super Bowl in 2006 and Tomlin was an afterthought at the start of this process. Pittsburgh had two in-house candidates that they were also interviewing—their offensive coordinator, Ken Wisenhunt, and Russ Grimm, their offensive line coach. Many people thought that one of these coaches would get the job.

The Steelers interviewed each candidate two times and the 34-year-old Tomlin could only get their attention and, ultimately the job, if he was a different, big-upside, strong-willed leader who had a better chance to be a great coach than the incumbents. After the interviews, the Pittsburgh owners judged that the underdog with the big dream was the guy who could produce big results.

Tomlin got the job. He led Pittsburgh to a division title in his first season as a head coach. In his second season, the Steelers were Super Bowl champions. Mike Tomlin has said, "The one common bond that the really successful people I've met have is they are ridiculous dreamers. I am a ridiculous dreamer. Continue to dream. Don't let the reality of the world diminish those dreams." This Steel City coach is definitely someone who practices what he preaches.

J.K. Rowling
From Welfare to Wizards to Wealthy

In 1990, on a train trip from Manchester to London, Joanne Rowling's idea for a boy attending a wizardry school formed in her mind. After reaching her apartment, she began to jot down these ideas.

Shortly after this time, she moved to Portugal to teach English. She got married and had a daughter in July 1993. By November, she and her husband had separated. The next month she and her daughter moved to be close to her sister in Scotland.

In order to teach in Scotland, "Jo" had to earn a post-graduate certificate of education. To obtain this certificate, she had to take a full-time, yearlong course. She began this course in August of 1995 after writing her first novel while living off welfare support.

After completing her manuscript, *Harry Potter and the Philosopher's Stone,* Christopher Little Literary Agents represented Rowling in her search to find a publisher. Twelve publishing companies rejected her manuscript until Bloomsbury, a small publishing company in London, accepted it. Although Bloomsbury agreed to publish the book, Rowling's editor advised her to get a day job since she had little chance of making much money from a children's book.

I guess the editor underestimated the potential of this children's book. After seven books and many items related to these books, the Harry Potter brand is now worth an estimated $15 billion. In addition, these stories sparked a love of reading in many children. It's a good thing this single mom surviving on welfare kept her dream alive.

Jim Tomsula

From Carpet Salesman to Coaching on the Sidelines

When Jim Tomsula graduated from Catawba College he did not want to be a football coach. He wanted "to be a businessman and earn the big bucks." So, that is what he did and he did it well. Soon after graduating from college, Tomsula lived in a two-story home on two acres overlooking Lake Norman in North Carolina.

It didn't take him long to realize the business world was not for him. He missed football and the feeling of belonging to a team. His wife, Julie, knew he wasn't satisfied and convinced him to get into coaching. With this urging, Tomsula took an assistant coach job at his alma mater that paid only $731 a month.

During this coaching stint, Jim and Julia had their first two children. After the children came, Tomsula felt he was not providing for his family the way he wanted. The family packed up and moved to Pittsburgh and Tomsula got back into business. A few years later, sensing his unhappiness, Julie once again convinced her husband to get back into coaching.

This time it was not as easy. Tomsula could only find an unpaid position back at Catawba. While his family lived with relatives, Jim slept in his car, attended coaches' meetings in the morning, sold carpet in the afternoon and went back to campus at night for practice.

In 1998, Lionel Taylor, the head coach of NFL Europe's London Monarchs, called Tomsula and offered him a job coaching the defensive line. After consulting his family, he took this job. Tomsula ended up working for four different NFL Europe teams and eventually became the head coach of the Rhein Fire in 2006. Even after getting these coaching jobs overseas, he returned to coach Catawba every off-season. Over those nine years, his family split their time between hotels in Europe and houses in North Carolina. His children would start the school year in the States and finish it in Europe.

In 2007, the NFL closed its European league. The Tomsulas moved back to the States for good. Jim got hired by the San Francisco 49ers as a defensive line coach. He coached in this position for over three years before being named the 49ers interim head coach on December 27, 2010, after the team fired its former head coach Mike Singletary. Under Tomsula's leadership, the 49ers defeated the Arizona Cardinals 38–7 in his first game as head coach. I don't think even Tomsula could have dreamed of this while he was sleeping in his car and selling flooring.

This story has a personal connection for me. I attended Catawba College—a small Division 3 school—for a semester in 1996. In addition, one of my best friends from childhood played football at Catawba and was coached by Tomsula during his time there. We recently spoke and I asked him about Coach Tomsula. He said that Jim was very passionate about coaching and was not surprised at his success.

Acknowledgements

I first must thank my most amazing wife, Tracy. Thank you so much for being the greatest wife and mother a husband could ask for. Your unconditional love and support mean the world to me. I cherish every day I spend with you.

Ava and Ella: You are the greatest gifts a daddy could ask for. I love you both with all of my heart.

Mom, Dad, Meno and Art: Thank you all for the wonderful examples you have set for me. You have shown me the true definition of being rich.

To the Roadshow Crew: Thank you for dreaming big and allowing me to share this wonderful journey with you.

I would also like to thank the individuals that took time out of their busy schedules to read and endorse my book. Thank you Laura Adams, Dale Alexander, Gerri Detweiler, Rick Durkee, Bill Faiferlick, Donna Freedman, Neale Godfrey, Marilyn Hickey, Johnny Isakson, Samuel Jackson, Michael Kanell, Kimberly Palmer, Jason Price, Pat Robertson, Manisha Thakor, Juan Williams, Jeff Yeager and Martha Zoller—I am forever grateful for your kind words.

This list would not be complete without expressing my thanks to my publisher—Nancy Cleary. Your passion and excitement are contagious. Even though you have many other authors you treat me like I am your only one. You are such a joy to work with and make me feel so important! I am so blessed that God placed me in your path. Thank you so much for being so supportive of me and all that you have done.

Finally, to my other family members, my friends and my readers: Thank you for all of your support and guidance.

About the Author

Danny Kofke is currently a special education teacher in Georgia. His love of teaching and finances led him to write the book *How To Survive (and perhaps thrive) On A Teacher's Salary*. With more knowledge and information, Danny decided to pen this new book—*A Simple Book of Financial Wisdom: Teach Yourself (and Your Kids) How To Live Wealthy with Little Money*.

Danny has appeared on numerous television shows including *Fox & Friends*, CNN's *Newsroom*, *The 700 Club*, CNN's *Your Bottom Line*, Fox Business Network's *Follow The Money*, *ABC News Now*, FOX Business Network's *Varney & Company*, HLN's *The Clark Howard Show* and *MSNBC Live*. In addition, Danny has been interviewed on over 200 radio shows and featured in a number of publications including *USA Today*, Bankrate.com, *Parade*, *Instructor Magazine*, CBS MoneyWatch.com, CNN.com, FoxBusiness.com, *The Atlanta Journal Constitution*, *USA Weekend*, *The Wall Street Journal*, ABCNews.com, Yahoo Finance, *Woman's Day*, *Consumer's Digest*, *Bottom Line Personal*, *Your Family Today* and *The Huffington Post*.

A lot of people think that figuring out financial matters and investing are difficult and are intimidated by it. Danny wants to show others that if this 35-year-old school teacher can figure it out then they can too.

To learn more about Danny please visit:
DannyKofke.blogspot.com
Facebook.com/SimpleFinancial Wisdom
Twitter.com/DannyKofke

Index

CPSIA information can be obtained at www.ICGtesting.com
Printed in the USA
LVOW081458040312

271519LV00001B/45/P